Genetics and the Manipulation of Life

The Forgotten Factor of Context

Renewal in Science

*The Renewal in Science series offers books that seek to enliven
and deepen our understanding of nature and science.*

*The Wholeness of Nature: Goethe's Way toward a Science
of Conscious Participation in Nature**
by Henri Bortoft

*For a brief description see the last page of this book.

Genetics and the Manipulation of Life

The Forgotten Factor of Context

Craig Holdrege

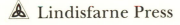 Lindisfarne Press

This publication was made possible through generous
support provided by the Fetzer Institute and
the Cultural Freedom Foundation

Figures 1 (page 12) and 2 (page 14), courtesy of Mathias Buess; Figures 6 (p. 28), 7 (p. 29), 8 (p. 30), and 9 (p. 32) from the Archive of the Natural Science Section Research Laboratory, Goetheanum, Dornach, Switzerland; Figures 10 (p. 36) and 11 (p. 39), reprinted from Jochen Bockemühl, *In Partnership with Nature* (1981, Wyoming, RI: Bio-Dynamic Literature); Figure 14 (page 50), Karl von Frisch, *Animal Architecture* (1974, New York and London: Harcourt Brace Javonovich), p. 103; Figure 15 (page 64), from A.G. Bearn and J. L. German III, "Chromosomes and Disease," *Scientific American*, vol. 205, no. 5, pp. 66–76; Figure 16 (page 98), courtesy of Professor Lynn Margulis, *Sciencewriters*; Figure 17 (page 103), cover photograph from *MPG Spiegel* (3/91), Goettingen, Germany; Figure 19 (page 141), Catherine Parker Anthony and Norma Jane Kolthoff, *Anatomy and Physiology* (1975, St. Louis: The C.V. Mosby Company), p. 86; Figures 20 (page 141), and 21 (page 142), Benninghof and Goerttler, *Lehrbuch der Anatomie des Menschen* (Bd.I, 13. Auflage, 1980), pp. 411 and 412.

Copyright © 1996, Craig Holdrege

Published by Lindisfarne Press
RR4 Box 94 A-1, Hudson, NY 12534

Library of Congress Cataloging-in-Publication Data
Holdrege, Craig, 1953–
    Genetics and the manipulation of life : the forgotten factor of context
/ Craig Holdrege.
       p.   cm. – (Renewal in science)
    Includes bibliographical references and index.
    ISBN 0-940262-77-0
    1. Genetics—Philosophy. 2. Nature and nurture. I. Title. II. Series.
QH430.H65   1996
575.1'01–dc20   96–9542
                                                     CIP

10 9 8 7 6 5 4 3 2 1

CONTENTS

For my children

(Daddy, are you still writing that book?)

ACKNOWLEDGMENTS

Reading book acknowledgments, I always wonder how the authors know where to begin and where to stop thanking people. Now I am in the same position. It seems as though any boundary one draws is artificial, because, in a certain sense, one's whole life has served as preparation for writing a book.

Since high school I have struggled with the question of knowledge. Reading and studying philosophy and science, I found that philosophic discourse and scientific investigation formed two separate worlds. I was looking for a union of the two—a more self-reflective science. Fortunately, I discovered the works of Rudolf Steiner (1983, 1986, 1988), and then also of Goethe (1988) and Owen Barfield (1965). These thinkers, especially Steiner, have given me the possibility of exercising my thinking to break through prevailing habits of thought. I am deeply indebted to them.

When I was a student in Europe, Jochen Bockemühl, the former director of the scientific research laboratory at the Goetheanum in Dornach, Switzerland, helped me to begin looking at heredity and genetics in a new way. His love of phenomena, coupled with a penetrating clarity of thought, remain an inspiration to me. In the past ten years

I have discussed and worked on questions of heredity and genetic engineering with Johannes Wirz. Many of the ideas in this book were developed in our conversations. During all the years of working on this theme, Henrike Holdrege, my wife, has always been willing to think things through with me. I can't imagine the book without her.

I am indebted to the many high school students I have worked with for the past sixteen years. They have taught me to present material in a more understandable way, and their questions often help me to look at things with fresh eyes.

The various versions of the manuscript, or parts thereof, have gone through the hands and minds of many people. I would like to thank them all for taking the time to read and comment on the manuscript: John Barnes, Ron Brady, Malcolm Gardner, Henrike Holdrege, Thomas Locker, Lynn Margulis, Joel Morrow, David Seamon, Stephen Talbott, Johannes Wirz, and Arthur Zajonc.

The section on the cow in chapter 6 appeared in *The Threefold Review* (Winter/Spring, 1996, pp. 11–14); I thank the editors, Joel Kobran and Gary Lamb, for their thorough critique. My thanks to Steffen Schneider for sharing his practical knowledge of cows with me.

It was a rewarding and invigorating experience to work with an editor, Stephen Talbott, who understood what I was trying to say and helped me to say it better. My thanks to John Barnes and Christopher Bamford of Lindisfarne Press for their interest and effort in getting the book published.

I have been able to do research and to write this book because I have teaching-free periods during the school year. Financial support has been provided through the Goethean Science Fund, initiated by Henry Barnes and

Kathleen Young, who were also instrumental in my receiving grants from the Cultural Freedom Foundation, the Emil Buehler Foundation, the Mahle-Stiftung, and the Waldorf Schools Fund. I have also received grants from the Future Value Fund. My thanks to the individuals in those institutions who have seen value in this work, and also to my colleagues at the Hawthorne Valley School for accepting my periods of absence.

FIGURE 1. A basswood tree.
(Drawing by Mathias Buess; printed in Bockemühl, 1992.)

A Tree without a Landscape

The tree in figure 1 probably does not match your picture of a typical healthy basswood, or linden tree. The trunk is long and narrow; it does not branch until the top. The "crown" is small in comparison with the trunk.

Is this tree not healthy? Is it the remnant of a dying forest? No. It is perfectly healthy, but it is shown out of context. Standing in the middle of a forest, it looks like most of the other trees on the north-facing slope of a forested valley in Switzerland. The rocky forest floor is covered with moss and ferns. Even in the summer it is dark and damp, and one's eyes follow the long trunks upward to the canopy of green, through which only small patches of sky are visible. The single basswood is part of the "super-tree" we call the forest.

On the opposite side of the valley basswoods also grow, but how differently (figure 2). Here on the dry and exposed south-facing slope they appear almost bushlike. There is no single trunk, and the "crown" unfolds immediately above the ground.

Organisms teach us that we begin to understand isolated facts only when we look at them in the light of a larger context. Indeed, facts are isolated only because we make them so in order to focus more clearly and narrowly. Through understanding we overcome the isolation, re-creating the context in which life gains its fullness.

FIGURE 2. Basswood on south-facing slope.
(Drawing by Mathias Buess; printed in Bockemühl, 1992.)

I take context seriously in this book. In considering any given phenomenon, experiment, or thought, I attempt to describe the context out of which it has arisen, so that the reduced focus finds its complement in a larger horizon. Gaining a broader perspective entails a shift in our way of looking at things, a shift in which the whole process of knowing becomes just as essential as any isolated object of knowledge. Only then do we begin to understand what it means to be an organism. Chapter 1 leads us into the process of contextual understanding.

Although it may sound simple to restore context in order to gain understanding, it is not. Our contrary habits run deep. In science we are trained to seek the clear outlines of decisive facts held in sharp focus. We learn to look for underlying mechanisms—material causes—by excluding from view the ambiguities of any larger view. This approach is called reductionism, and it is taught, if not always by name, in schools and universities around the world.

For example, in pursuing the physiological mechanisms that cause the basswood's trunk to grow long and narrow, we study cell growth. This leads to cell metabolism. Finally, we may discover genes associated with cell proliferation or elongation. Such a study is perfectly justified and leads to detailed knowledge.

But problems arise when we forget the limitations imposed upon our conclusions by the narrowness of our focus. Our answers are valid only within the boundaries of our chosen methods and perspectives. We have not, after all, explained the basswood's form when we determine some of the physiological parameters of cell growth. If we believe we have, then we have lost sight of the basswood growing in a north-slope forest community. Outside this context the physiological processes associated with elongation simply do not occur. Unfortunately, it is unlikely today that a scientist studying genes will know very much about the way a basswood grows on a northern or southern slope. The requirements of specialization leave little time for cultivating the contextually rich knowledge of an organism in its different natural settings.

If we cannot fully understand an organism without its environment, neither can we understand genes without organisms. Genes are usually treated as independent agents, causing the organism's traits. The all-powerful gene loses something of its mystique when, having first looked at it as we looked at the isolated basswood, we then restore its context. I attempt this restoration in chapters 2 through 5.

Along the way we will examine the origin and development of heredity theories, experiments, and observations. Carefully following the path of rigorous, reductionist genetics, we will acknowledge its achievements, its boundaries, and its inflated claims.

It will become clear along our journey that genetics as a body of results is inseparable from genetics as a prior way of thinking. Science is often naively construed as dealing with phenomena that, in their essential nature, have nothing to do with human consciousness. Yet, our understanding of things inevitably reflects the conceptual framework, narrow or broad, that we bring to the phenomena. As we will see, the framework quite literally *is* part of the truly recognized phenomenon. One of the decisive challenges of modern science is to overcome the barrier—constructed only in recent centuries—between the mental and the sense perceptible.

Moreover, genetic engineering is no mere theoretical doctrine. It has become a powerful agent of change. The geneticist interacts with the organisms under investigation, subjecting them to willful interpretations and premeditated actions. Are we willing to accept the implications of this? Do we understand the organisms we manipulate and the consequences of these manipulations? Can we accept responsibility for our actions if they are based on a reduced view of life and organisms? I will deal with such questions in chapters 5 and 6.

Surely the attempts to reshape life on Earth require us to seek the broadest possible context of understanding. And unless that context is large enough to include the human being, not only as knower but also as doer and creator, we can only blindly follow our technical capabilities wherever they chance to lead.

We human beings are clearly the effectors of genetic manipulation, but we have also become objects of this technology. In chapter 6 I suggest the difficulties involved in understanding human heredity. Any purely genetic consideration of the human being becomes inhuman by virtue of its narrowness. And yet, many are hailing the Human Genome Project as if its technically remarkable gene-mapping accomplishments held the key to a final and full understanding of the human being.

Will genetic technology take on a life of its own? The contextual approach urged here can help prevent this. By reckoning with the human being as an integral part of every scientific endeavor, we can begin to fathom what it means to accept responsibility both for the act of knowing and for the future we create on the basis of our knowledge.

CHAPTER ONE

A Contextual Approach to Plant Heredity

Now let us try to recover a landscape for the isolated basswood.

Almost everyone today "knows" that heredity is a mechanism for passing traits from parent to offspring, and that genes determine traits. We are taught that genes and the mechanisms of heredity are essentially the same in all organisms. We can follow the almost daily reports of new discoveries—genes for various cancers, genes for assorted mental illnesses, even genes for behavioral traits.

To free oneself from these pictures of heredity demands considerable exertion. But this is what I am asking you to do: to discard for the moment the conceptual framework of conventional genetics, and to look with fresh eyes at seemingly simple phenomena.

In discussing the plant, I will not speak of genes, traits, adaptation, or competition. I want to lead you into a different way of looking and thinking. I will describe plants and experiments in a fairly detailed way. I ask you to look discerningly at the illustrations, and not to jump immediately to the discussions based on them. By looking and thinking through what you see, you will begin to develop concepts that enliven the phenomena. Such concepts are richer, although at times more elusive, than many of the abstractions we carry around with us.

The Plant and Its Environment

Imagine walking out in the springtime onto a grassy yard with a flower garden. The yard is bordered by a deciduous forest through which a path leads. At one place in the woods there is an opening in the canopy, and in this clearing the undergrowth is denser and lusher. The dandelions are in bloom.

We also see many dandelions growing in the grass of the yard. If we look more closely, we observe that the leaves lie nearly prostrate, and that a very short stalk carries the flower head to the height of the tips of the grass blades (figure 3a).

Only a short distance away, much larger dandelions are growing as weeds in the flower bed (figure 3b). The leaves are nearly upright; the flower stalks are long and thin.

In the clearing in the woods nearby, the dandelions are even larger, not only the leaves, but also the flower heads (figure 3c). We also notice the markedly broad leaf blades, especially in the more rounded distal (outermost) lobes. These large plants are, however, easier to dig out of the earth than the more firmly rooted dandelions growing in the yard.

Each leaf portrayed in figure 4 was taken from a different dandelion and represents the largest leaf on its plant. All plants grew within seventy meters of each other. The variety of sizes and forms is quite astounding. The very

a : Yard

b : Garden

c : Forest

FIGURE 3. Three specimens of dandelion (*Taraxacum officinale*).
Each specimen grew in a different microhabitat. (One eighth of natural size.)

small yard leaves (a) stand in contrast to the large forest-clearing leaves (d). The one huge leaf (d4, measured at twenty-three and one half inches long) was picked two years later than the other leaves, a year in which the forest-clearing specimens as a whole were larger; even in this year it was an extreme example.

The other leaves from the forest clearing are fairly uniform, as also are the yard leaves. We can, therefore, reasonably relate the overall differences between the two groups to their respective microhabitats—that is, to the influence of their environments.

The leaves in b and c lie, with respect to size, between the first two groups. Moreover, the leaves in both b and c show more variation among themselves. Perhaps their microhabitats—patio cracks in southern and northern exposure—are themselves less uniform. (For example, cracks may vary in width.) But even if such fine environmental variations are evidenced in the size and form of the leaves, one can readily imagine that at least some of the difference—between, say, the short, broad, rounded leaves (c2) and the long, narrow, pointed leaves (c3)—is due to something else. This something else could be heredity.

If we now imagine one of these plants producing seeds that are dispersed by the wind, we may correctly suppose that the offspring will develop according to the conditions in each different microhabitat. The seeds from the small-leafed yard plants will not develop into tiny forest-clearing plants; we find no such plants in forest clearings.

All of this can be demonstrated quite clearly. While we cannot easily follow the transmission of seeds in nature, we can perform experiments that help us to see what goes on. Many experiments have in fact been done, and I will

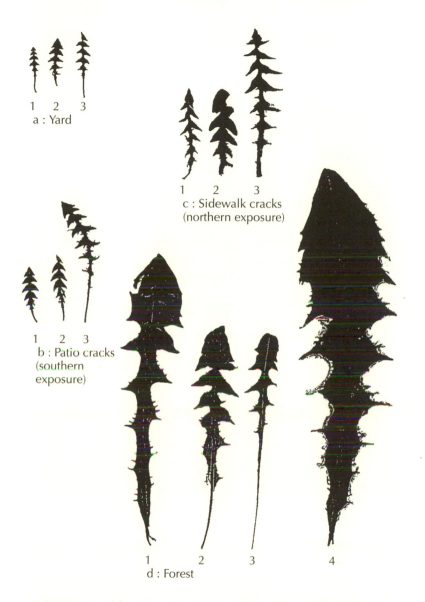

FIGURE 4. Dandelion leaves. Each leaf was taken from a different specimen. The leaves in each group (a–d) were taken from plants growing in the same micro-habitat. (Pressed leaves, one sixth of natural size.)

describe Gaston Bonnier's classic experiments from the end of the nineteenth century (discussed in Schroeter, 1926).

Bonnier was a French scientist interested in understanding how plants grow under different environmental conditions. For this purpose, he cut young specimens of many different species in half lengthwise and planted one half in an alpine garden (two thousand meters above sea level) and the other half in a garden near Paris (thirty-two meters). The drawings (figure 5) show the marked differences that developed when each half-plant became a whole plant in its new environment. Every part of the plant—down to details of cellular structure—changed. The root system was strongly developed in the alpine plants, while the leaves remained small and only one or two flower heads formed. By contrast, the lowland plants showed less extensive root systems in relation to their lusher top growth. Whereas the lowland scabious developed many side stems, the alpine scabious did not branch at all.

Equally remarkable is the similarity between the exemplars of different species in the same environment. This shows us that there is a general and not just a species-defined plasticity in plants. At the same time, this similarity points to the major effect of the environment upon plant form.

The Rooted Plant

Bonnier's experiments demonstrate the immense plasticity of plants. The plant is open to its environment, developing form and function in harmony with it. The environment draws out, so to speak, the plant's potential. More narrowly circumscribed experiments can help us see how a

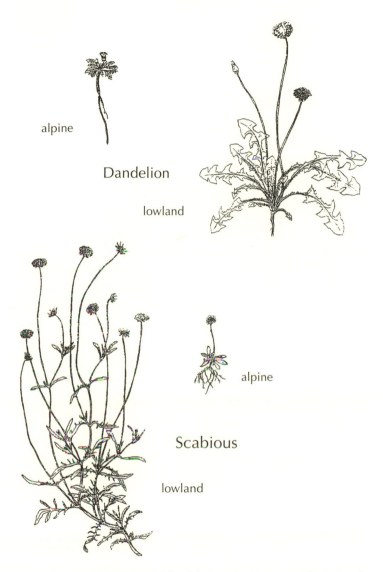

FIGURE 5. Young specimens of dandelion and scabious (*Scabiosa lucida*) were cut in half lengthwise; the half specimens were planted in alpine and in lowland gardens respectively. The drawings depict the plants in the flowering stage; all plants are drawn to the same scale (after Bonnier, from Schroeter, 1926).

particular element of the environment is revealed in a plant's growth and structure.

I will take the example of soil.[1] Three plants of different species were grown in two different types of soil: composted garden soil and a one-to-one mixture of sand and loam. The garden soil was dark brown and loose, while the sand-loam soil was denser and heavier. The plants were grown in specially designed boxes that allow the observation of root growth (Bockemühl, 1969). The three plant species are all annuals, but belong to different families—groundsel (*Senecio vulgaris*, composite family), rape (*Brassica napus*, mustard family) and broad bean (*Vicia faba*, pea family).

Figures 6, 7, and 8 show the progressive development of these three species grown in sand-loam soil and in composted garden soil. The plants in the sand-loam soil are markedly less differentiated than those in the garden soil. The contrast becomes visible soon after germination. The primary roots grow straight downward through the sand-loam, with little branching, while in the garden soil they immediately begin to form many lateral roots.

This tendency endures in the further course of development. The roots in sand-loam form long lateral roots, but these in turn branch minimally. The whole root body is simple and regular. By contrast, the root body in garden soil appears more irregular, due to the abundant branching of the roots. The garden soil plants penetrate the soil much more intensively than the sand-loam plants.

---

1. This is unpublished research material from the Natural Science Section, Goetheanum, Dornach, Switzerland. It is used with permission.

The top parts of the roots of the broad bean and rape in garden soil thicken considerably in the course of development, while they remain thin in sand-loam. Also, the broad bean has a symbiotic relationship with nitrogen-fixing bacteria in its roots. The roots form so-called nodules, which house the bacteria. In garden soil, the broad bean produces more nodules—and larger ones—than in sand-loam.

The difference between the roots is mirrored in the plant tops. The plants growing in sand-loam soil develop a main, vertical stem with almost no lateral branches. The garden soil plants ramify much more vigorously. Groundsel and broad bean are bushy in appearance, due to the many stems that branch off the main stem. Rape branches only at the top, but is, in comparison with its sand-loam relative, large and robust.

Figure 9 shows the leaves from the main stem of each plant. The leaves were pressed before they wilted and were then arranged in the order of their appearance—the earliest leaves to the left of each row, the latest leaves to the right. We see the same tendency in the leaves as we do in the other parts of the plant. The leaves are considerably smaller in sand-loam soil. Moreover, the leaf form of groundsel and rape is simpler in this soil. By comparison, these species produce more differentiated leaves in garden soil, a fact clearly visible in the numerous, small, finely cut lobes of the leaf blade. Broad bean varies less, which is characteristic of the pea family.

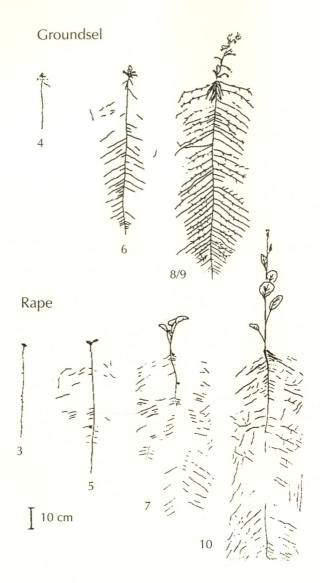

Groundsel

Rape

FIGURE 6. Plants grown in sand-loam soil. The number under the roots indicates the age of the plant in weeks. All plants are drawn to the same scale. (From the Archive of the Natural Science Section Research Laboratory, Goetheanum, Dornach, Switzerland.)

Groundsel

Rape

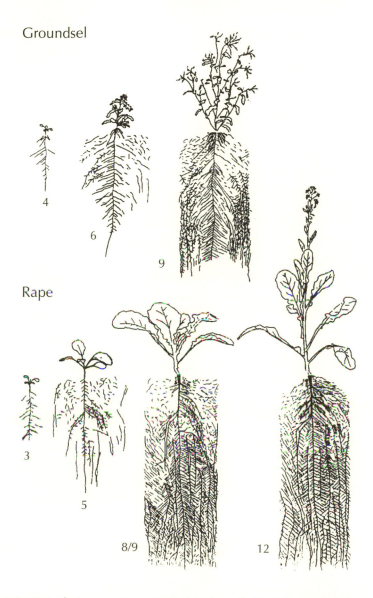

FIGURE 7. Plants grown in composted garden soil. (For further explanation see text and Figure 6.)

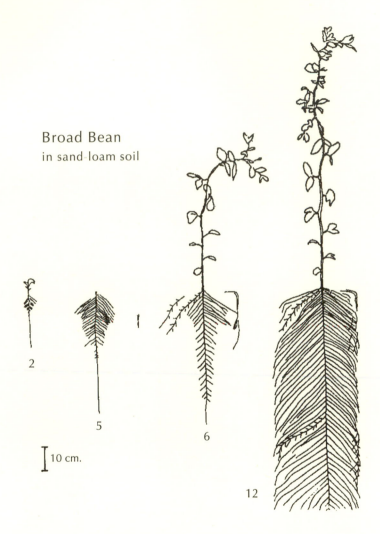

Broad Bean

in sand-loam soil

2

5

6

10 cm.

12

FIGURE 8. Broad bean grown in sand-loam soil (above) and composted garden soil (opposite page). The number under the roots indicates the age of the plant in weeks. All plants are drawn to the same scale.

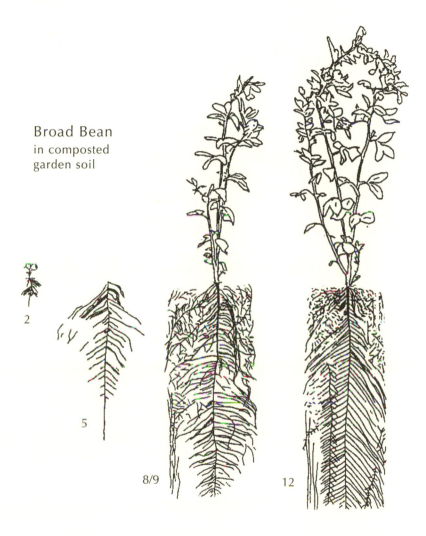

Broad Bean
in composted
garden soil

(From the Archive of the Natural Science Section Research Laboratory, Goetheanum, Dornach, Switzerland.)

Groundsel

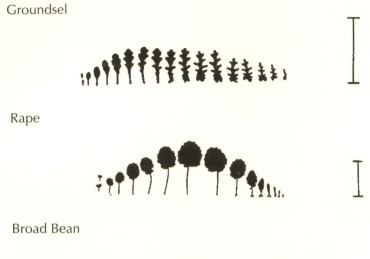

Rape

Broad Bean

SAND-LOAM SOIL

FIGURE 9. Each of the six rows of leaves (above and opposite pages) represents all the leaves of the main stem of one plant. The three plants above grew in sand-loam soil. The three plants on the opposite page grew in composted garden soil. Scale bar: 10 cm.

Learning from the Plant

What can we learn from these experiments? First, although all three plants are members of different families, each relates to the environment in a similar way. The environment draws forth the same tendency in each plant. Or to put it another way, the same environment is clearly revealed in each species. Of course, a swamp plant will probably not find the conditions necessary to sustain its growth in a desert, but if it were able to grow, it would take on characteristics similar to other desert species.

Groundsel

Rape

Broad Bean

COMPOSTED GARDEN SOIL

(From the Archive of the Natural Science Section Research Laboratory, Goetheanum, Dornach, Switzerland.)

Second, the plant as a whole reflects its environmental conditions as a whole. Not only do the roots grow differently in different soils, but every other part of the plant as well. Each part expresses the different conditions in its own way, yet overall growth tendencies are the same in every part—the roots and stem show little branching and the leaf form remains simple in sand-loam soil; the roots and stems differentiate through stronger branching and the leaves are more distinctly lobed in garden soil. So the soil conditions are revealed throughout the whole.

We might consider the conditions of sand-loam soil to be poorer for these plants, since growth in this medium is not as vigorous and differentiated. Nonetheless, these plants go through all stages of development in a modified form, that is, in a manner corresponding to the conditions.

We are a long way from an exhaustive understanding of the concept of the organism as a whole. But we at least have a starting point: the plant organism as a whole is not merely an agglomeration of parts. It is not a machine-like collection of externally assembled pieces. The parts emerge or grow out of the germinal organism and reflect the way in which the organism as a whole relates to its environment. While the roots, in direct contact with the soil, change according to the soil type, so does every other part in a similar way. The part serves the whole, but the whole also lives in every part.

Furthermore, we can form a concrete concept of the relationship of a plant to its environment. We all know that light, air, water, and soil are necessary conditions for plant growth. But when we observe how differently plants grow in different soils, then we are learning not only about the plant's plasticity, but also about the nature of the soil. So if we want to know what belongs to the plant's environment, we must study the plant itself. We do not, however, study it as an isolated entity, but rather as an organism that reveals through itself a larger context. The three plants tell us about garden soil and sand-loam soil through the way they grow in these soils.

Soil as environment of a plant is a relational concept; it is not a wholly self-contained thing. The same holds for all other so-called environmental factors. Likewise in the reverse direction: we understand the plant only when we look through it and "see," for example, the soil.

Considering organisms in this way is the heart of a contextual approach. It is an approach modeled after the life of the plant itself. No plant exists in a vacuum. It grows and develops in a context, without which it cannot exist. The environment, as relation, is inseparable from the idea of the plant.

In order to be clear about the relational nature of the concept of environment, it is helpful (although at times terminologically cumbersome) to distinguish between surroundings and environment. Surroundings include all that we find literally around the organism; they embrace the spatial relations that all physical objects have. Environment goes beyond the spatial to include functional relations. When looking at environmental relations, we consider organisms as beings of interaction, and not merely as things in space.

The odor given off by a skunk cabbage clearly belongs to the environment of the flies and bees that are attracted to it. Whether the odor belongs to the environment of the birch tree growing nearby is much less certain.

The Plant in Time

In the beginning of May the seeds of the field poppy (*Papaver rhoes*) begin to germinate. The tiny seed breaks open and a fine root tip grows out of the seed and down into the soil. The primary growth of a seedling is in its roots. As the seed leaves (cotyledons) unfold, the main root continues its downward growth and begins to branch.

After three weeks the poppy has grown a few small leaves (figure 10), which have long stalks and simple, rounded blades. New leaves continue to form and unfold. Once a leaf unfolds, it hardly grows any more. Each new leaf is larger than its predecessor. Five weeks after germination

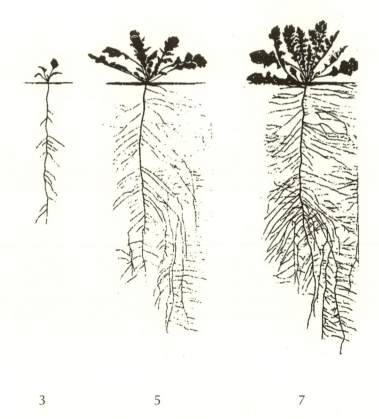

3   5   7

FIGURE 10. Development of a field poppy (*Papaver rhoes*). The numbers under the roots indicate the age of the plant in weeks (from Bockemühl, 1981).

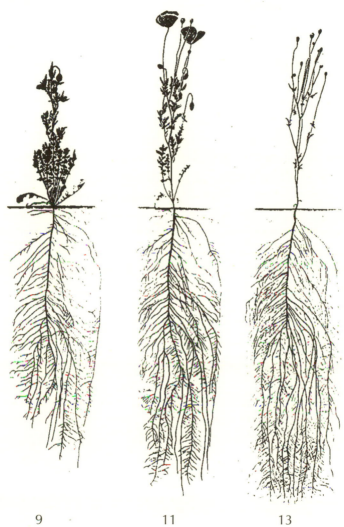

9   11   13

the poppy has a many-leaved rosette. Many lateral roots branch off the long taproot.

At seven weeks the leaf rosette has become even fuller. The newest leaves in the middle of the rosette stand almost upright and are more finely differentiated than the older, peripheral leaves. Some of these older leaves lie prostrate and are dying—they lose their chlorophyll and turn brown. The first leaves begin to die when the plant is only a few weeks old. None of the leaves present in the three-week-old poppy are still part of the seven-week-old plant.

Up to this point a casual observer might confuse the poppy with a dandelion, since both form rosettes. But the poppy now undergoes a marked transformation. A vertical stem begins to grow out of the rosette. This stem elongates and also carries leaves, which are smaller and more deeply cut than the rosette leaves. The higher up the vertical stem, the smaller the leaves become (figure 11).

At the base of each leaf is a small, axillary (lateral) bud. The buds of the uppermost leaves swell and become rounded flower buds. The stalks of these flower buds grow, so that at nine weeks we observe extended flower stalks carrying the drooping buds—a characteristic feature of poppies.

The flower stalk straightens, the bud leaves open and fall off, and the scarlet red petals unfold. These brilliant petals are short lived, but since the buds open one after another, the poppy remains in flower for about two weeks.

The eleven-week-old poppy has flower buds, flowers, and the first fruit capsules containing the developing seeds. The visible plant has reached a stage of maximal differentiation. This is also true of the roots, culminating in a finely branched rooting body. In the meantime all of the rosette leaves have died.

FIGURE 11. Leaves of the main stem of a field poppy (*Papaver rhoes*). Sepals and petals are included at the top (from Bockemühl, 1981).

Only two weeks after the high point of flowering, the poppy is reduced to a mere skeleton. The leaves and flowers are dead. The dying stalks remain as an afterimage of the earlier branching growth. Root development has ceased. The fruit capsules, now drying out, each contain hundreds of tiny hard seeds. Only the innermost core of each seed—the germ—remains alive.

So the one poppy plant disintegrates into myriad seeds. Each of the seeds is the first stage of a new poppy plant. When these seeds are released from the fruits and fall to the ground, some may germinate soon thereafter. Others may remain dormant through the winter and germinate in the following spring. The cycle begins anew.

Approaching the Plant with Fluid Thinking

This description of the poppy shows us how the plant is continually changing—producing new forms as the old ones die off. When I observe any given phase in the plant's development, I have only a fleeting time-slice of the plant before me. The plant is never whole in space; the whole is created in time. Living in time, the plant successively pours its forms into space. What I see are, in a sense, the cast-off products of development; the developmental process as such is invisible. The "time-body" of the plant engenders its "spatial body."

The plant leads us out of space and into time. This fact places special demands on our thinking. If we consider, for example, the rows of leaves, then we can initially grasp each leaf as an entity in space (see figures 9 and 11). Each individual leaf has its own clearly defined form, which can be drawn or photographed. This is the leaf as an object.

But the row of leaves is only a dead picture of the plant's development. To come nearer to the life of the plant, we must go beyond the leaf as isolated object. The first step is to realize that each leaf is part of a whole sequence of leaves. It is isolated neither in space nor in time. We then recognize a pattern in the sequence of leaves. The first leaves are small with rounded blades. Then the leaf stalk grows longer and the leaf as a whole grows larger. Differentiation begins, and as it continues, the size of the leaf begins to decrease. The last leaves are small, with sharp, linear outlines.

In order to speak of transformation we go beyond the individual leaves and view them as fragmentary expressions of a process. We can only grasp this transformation process in our thinking, guided by the perceptible phenomena. There is no individual form that is at the same time the process. We must, in our thinking, connect one form with the next. This is possible only when our thinking does not get stuck in the fixed contours of each single leaf. To move from form to form, we must dissolve the fixed contours in our minds. When we do this, the plant as process becomes recognizable.

Each leaf is formed out of a primordial bud of embryonic tissue that bears no resemblance to the finished leaf. The primordium begins to differentiate, and when the leaf unfolds it is essentially complete. In the meantime the plant has begun to bring forth the next leaf—a leaf that has a different form from its predecessor. The leaf emerges out of a temporal context and then stands in the spatial context of the other unfolded leaves.

The process of knowledge must proceed in the reverse direction. We begin with the end product—the plant in space. We pass from the spatial to the temporal transformation when we connect form with form in the sense of creating a mental transition from one leaf to the next. To come to the undifferentiated state—the origin of form—we must dissolve all set contours.

This is very difficult, because clear-cut forms are the normal anchors of mental clarity. But if we consciously dissolve the contours in thinking while managing to remain focused and precise, then our thinking follows a formed movement. Thinking must gain a fluid quality before it can grasp temporal processes as such, just as it must recognize crisp boundaries when dealing with spatial forms. To "move with" the organism's ability to produce manifold forms out of an undifferentiated state, we must bring plasticity and movement into our own thinking.

We make use of both capacities—the spatial and the temporal—at all times. Science clearly cultivates what I will call spatial thinking or object-thinking. It uses, but does not cultivate, what I will call fluid thinking, the kind of thinking that, already two centuries ago, Johann Wolfgang von Goethe urged upon the scientist: "If we wish to arrive at a living perception [*Anschauung*] of nature, we must make ourselves as mobile and flexible as nature herself, following the example she sets forth." (Goethe, 1977, p. 48; my translation.)

In the previous section we discussed how the plant relates as a whole to its environment. Now we see that the plant's response as a unified whole to its environment continues in a unified way through time.

From the moment the seed germinates, the plant is embedded in its environment. The root grows toward the midpoint of the Earth, following gravity (positive geotropism). The shoot grows in the opposite direction, away from the Earth's midpoint (negative geotropism). The specific features of the environment then become manifest in the plant's growth—minimal root branching in sand-loam, rich branching in garden soil. The quality of the soil is then also revealed in the form of each and every leaf. It is truly remarkable how the plant grows through its successive stages, while at every moment and in every part, declaring in a unified manner, the qualities of its environment.

Even if we can distinguish between light, water, and soil as isolated factors under experimental conditions, the plant as a unity displays the environmental conditions as a unity. In object-thinking we may properly consider individual factors, but the life of the plant reveals its environment in time, as a whole.

Inheritance: Plasticity and Limitation

Once, after discussing the dandelion in a class, I asked my students: what is inherited? A student responded: nothing! This is a fascinating answer. Other students responded by saying the form or structure of the plant is inherited. But the first student held fast to his answer, because he had seen that the form, size, and color of each plant vary in time and according to the environment. He therefore concluded that *nothing* fixed could be inherited—that is, no *thing* is inherited. He had gone beyond object-thinking in his conception of heredity.

The openness of the plant to its surroundings precludes fixity. The plant could not develop and, in developing, relate to the specific conditions of its surroundings if it were fixed and rigidly determined. The capacity to develop out of an undetermined state lies at the basis of heredity.

But if plasticity were the only aspect of heredity, then all plants in a given habitat would be almost identical, reflecting the environmental context. In reality, heredity as potential or plasticity is complemented by heredity as limitation or specificity.

Figure 12 shows two specimens of the same species, groundsel, growing under the same conditions. We are surprised to learn that they are plants of the same species, since the leaves are so different.

Let us look at the differences between the two plants more carefully. Variety V (I will explain the meaning of "variety" below) produces many leaves. The leaves are highly differentiated in the middle of the row. The blade is divided into many long, narrow lobes that extend from the leaf's midrib. In contrast, the leaves of variety Y are much more compact in appearance. The lobes remain short, and the indentations between them do not extend all the way into the midrib. Whereas the middle (differentiation) phase is accentuated in variety V, the final phase of contraction toward the stem is accentuated in variety Y.

If these contrasts do not express environmental differences, then in what context are they understandable? This becomes clearer when we learn that the two specimens developed from seeds borne by different plants. The origin of the seed is evidently crucial. When one sows the seeds that come from only one specimen of groundsel, then all progeny are almost identical in appearance (Bockemühl, 1972; Holdrege, 1986).

Such observations lead to the discovery that groundsel produces seeds either without any fertilization (agamospermy) or by self-fertilization (autogamy). This is, by the way, also the case with dandelions and with a fair number

of other flowering plants. The more typical cross-fertiliza-
tion between members of a species is, with these plants, a
rarity.

What I call a "variety" is thus a population of a particular
species, groundsel in this instance, characterized first by its
particular morphology and, second, by its reproductive isolation from other varieties. (In genetic terms, each variety
is a clone.)

Evidently the reproductive isolation is somehow connected to the morphological differences that we observe
between varieties. The problem is how to conceive of this
connection. We can at least say that as the plant is limited in the scope of its reproduction, so is it also limited
in the scope of its plasticity. Two specimens of different
varieties will both develop in accordance with environmental conditions—their hereditary plasticity—but each
of them does so in its own limited fashion, according to
its own nature.

Figure 13 shows two other specimens of the same varieties of groundsel. While the plants in figure 12 grew in a
northerly exposed greenhouse with diffuse daylight—that
is, without any direct sunlight—the plants in figure 13
grew in a greenhouse with direct sunlight. The seeds were
planted at the same time.

In direct sunlight, variety V takes on an appearance that
resembles variety Y in diffuse daylight. It produces fewer
leaves, and they are less differentiated and more compact.
Nonetheless, the leaves are not as contracted as in variety
Y—the leaf stalks and lobes are narrower and more elongated. Just such tendencies can be recognized as typical
for variety V even under varying conditions.

Variety Y varies much less in leaf form, although its
leaves are larger in direct sunlight than in diffuse light.

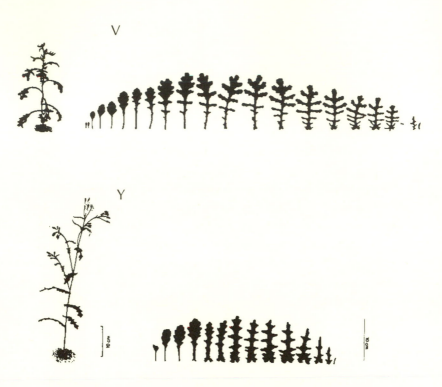

FIGURE 12. Two specimens of groundsel (*Senecio vulgaris*) grown under the same conditions in diffuse daylight. See text for explanation (from Holdrege, 1986).

This points to a general truth: under varying conditions it is easier to recognize a variety characterized by compact leaf forms than it is to recognize a variety with more differentiated leaves. The latter change more as conditions change. In other words, the form plasticity of a variety with differentiated leaves is greater than that of a variety with compact leaves.

Imagine that you are holding a groundsel seed in your hands before planting it. Depending on how, when, and

FIGURE 13. Two specimens of groundsel (*Senecio vulgaris*) grown under the same conditions in direct sunlight. See text for explanation (from Holdrege, 1986).

where you plant the seed, a limitless variety of forms can arise. All these potential forms are not, of course, stored in the seed. The concrete forms are emergent characteristics that arise out of a germinal state and develop in the interplay between the plant's plasticity and the environmental conditions. In particular surroundings the potential of the plant is evoked, but what appears is only one manifestation of the myriad ways in which this plant could develop.

The plasticity connected with the seed is, however, limited. The characteristic features of a variety (or, more generally, of any given species) are recognizable despite different conditions. There is something similar linking every generation. What is this something? It is a limited plastic tendency. This sounds abstract. It is, in fact, very difficult to find adequate words for what, in this case, stands before the mind's eye. It cannot be drawn and it cannot be adequately represented in any scheme or model.

The conception emerges only as we enliven the phenomena in thought. We follow the way a variety or species develops and varies in different conditions. Then we begin to form a fluid picture of the plant; it is no longer a clearly circumscribed object. When we then compare varieties or species, their unique characteristics become more evident. But this specific character is not something material or static that we can point to.

To be sure, we can identify a species by certain abstract characteristics. We can, for example, count the pistils and stamens, or the number of petals in a flower. To clearly discriminate one species from another, we typically employ such object-thinking. But mere classification by such means does not enable us to recognize the nature of the species plastically expressing itself in every plant characteristic. For that we need fluid, contextual thinking.

In sum, plant heredity has two fundamental components—plasticity and limitation or specificity. They are not separate, but we can distinguish them as the main colors in the spectrum of heredity. We can distinguish them, that is, when we study the plant in an environmental context. While each different environment invites a different expression of the plant (plasticity), the variability is bounded (limitation). The full range of expressions for any one species exhibits a restricted, specific character that is recognizably distinct from the expressions of a different species.

Organism-centered Concepts

We take for granted that a well-fed mouse will not grow to be the size of a cat, and that an underfed horse will not cease growing and live as a fox-sized horse. The limits on variation in size and shape are much more marked in animals than in plants. The hereditary boundaries are more fixed. But through their behavior, animals have a whole domain of plasticity related to a different kind of environment. Animals have a behavioral environment.

The behavioral environment is related to the structure and physiology of the animal's body. Karl von Frisch draws on certain species of ant to illustrate this (figure 14):

Some of the species of the genus *Colobopsis* build their nests in tree trunks and connect them to the outside world by a tiny hole which is only just large enough for one ant to pass through. Their community includes a not very numerous caste whose entire mission in life is to act as doorkeepers. They have enlarged heads, flattened in front, that fit exactly in the entrance hole so that they can function as live plugs. Moreover, the texture and color of the head, as far as it is visible from the outside, is such that it can hardly be distinguished from the surrounding bark. A doorkeeper will sit for hours in the entrance hole. She admits only members of her community demanding entrance by taps with their antennae, and these only if she can also recognize their smell. Should the hole be slightly larger than the head of the doorkeeper, the ants use a substance like papier-maché to narrow the entrance until it fits the head exactly. When the opening happens to be exceptionally large, several doorkeepers may block it jointly. (von Frisch, 1974, p. 103)

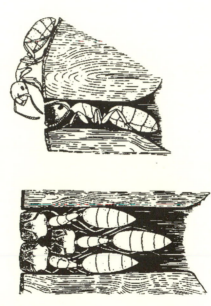

FIGURE 14. Ants belonging to the genus *Colobopsis*. See text for description (from von Frisch, 1974).

These extraordinary ants show how closely structure and behavior, form and function, can mesh. But even in this case of extreme specialization, there is nonetheless some minimal behavioral flexibility. The ant, perceiving when the entrance hole is too large for its head, alters its behavior to make the doorway smaller.

An animal always retains a certain degree of behavioral plasticity through which it deals with its ever changing surroundings. Take, for example, a certain mouse that was caught in a plastic, live-mouse trap. It gnawed a hole in the door of the trap, inserted its paw into the hole, pulled the door backward and upward, thereby opening it, and then quickly scampered out of the trap.

The surroundings were new to this mouse, and it responded to the novel situation. The specific sequence of events and certain particular actions, such as pulling up the door, had probably never occurred before in the mouse's life. But the *way* it escaped is typically "mouse"—limited and at the same time made possible by the body structure. The mouse gnawed with its large incisors, inserted its thin, long finger into the hole it created by gnawing, and so on.

So, in comparison with the plant, the animal possesses its own kind of openness to its surroundings—an openness expressed less through form than through behavior. Moreover, the concept of environment is lent a new dimension by animals and their behavior. Every creature warrants from us a modification of our concepts.

Organism-centered concepts must be allowed to grow and die like the organisms they are modeled after. They are not fixed definitions to which we hold fast. In other words, the contextual approach asks us to widen and deepen our concepts in every new context. The more differentiated and saturated our concepts become, the more they will enable us to approach the richness of the organisms themselves.

*   *   *

I have distinguished between different modes of thinking. Object-thinking sees clearly outlined and defined entities. The full thrust of object-thinking will become clearer in the following chapters. Fluid thinking grasps transformation, transcending the fixity of objects to follow process as such. Contextual thinking seeks relational understanding. It knows no isolated objects. The "things" of the world recede and relationships reveal themselves.

Against this background, I turn to Mendelian genetics.

CHAPTER TWO

The Path of Reduction: Mendel's Initial Steps

Mendelian Traits

Gregor Mendel (1822–1884) was a scientifically trained Catholic Priest. He lived in a monastery in Brno (in the present-day Czech Republic) and worked for many years as a science teacher in one of the city's schools, until he became the monastery's abbot. Mendel had an interest in plant breeding, which developed during his youth, and he oversaw and cared for the monastery's flower gardens.

This hobby became his scientific passion. Mendel hoped that by performing detailed breeding experiments he might find "a generally valid law for the formation and development of hybrids"—a law that had eluded other investigators until that time (Mendel, 1866). He succeeded. His success was based on great focus and concern for clarity, a clarity that included a conscious disregard for what did not fit into his experimental program. We will follow what Mendel discovered, but also what he did not take into account.

For eight years Mendel focused his scientific attention and activity on experimental breeding of varieties of the garden pea. For the purpose of his investigations he viewed the plants as if they were a collection of so-called characters, or traits. Such traits included the color of flowers or seeds, the form of seeds or fruits, the height of plants, and so on. Mendel then restricted his attention to certain traits. He stated at the beginning of his famous article of 1866 that traits such as the form or size of leaves must not be considered because they vary too much:

> Some of the traits listed do not permit a definite and sharp separation, since the difference rests on a 'more or less' which is often difficult to define. Such traits were not usable for individual experiments; these had to be limited to characteristics which stand out clearly and decisively in the plants. (Mendel, 1866)

Mendel used only characteristics possessing the clear, sharp edges demanded by his intellect. In his experiments, he had to find features varying so little that they remained crisply definable over the course of eight years. He found such relatively rigid characteristics: violet or white flowers, yellow or green seeds, round or angular seeds, and so on. These traits, belonging to living plants, do vary a bit, but Mendel ignored this fact; what was important to him was to be able to separate clearly, for example, violet from white, despite minor deviations.

In the previous chapter we discussed the plant's potential to change its form and structure in accordance with changing environmental conditions. Mendel excludes precisely this aspect of the plant from consideration. He "object-thinks" the plant. What becomes visible to fluid thinking, to a contextual approach, escapes the net of his investigations.

Mendel's approach is similar to watching a basketball game while attending only to the score—that is, noting only whether or not the ball passes through the hoop. For such a frame of mind, certain features of the game recede into the background—for example, whether the ball rolls around the rim before falling through the hoop, whether it is dunked or shot from thirty feet, whether one or the other team is "getting the bounces," whether each team is executing its strategy well. All these facets of the game, however, are still there to be viewed even when they are not attended to.

Likewise, Mendelian genetics rigorously ignores essential aspects of the organism's life. This is not "good" or "bad." It is a fact—a fact that tends to be overlooked. Presentations of Mendelian genetics usually do not clearly delineate the reduced field of phenomena he worked with. But this restriction is critical, because all subsequent explanations will pertain only to the reduced field.

Mendelian genetics explains what is visible to object-thinking when the organism is treated as a composite of clearly defined, unchanging traits. It does not penetrate to the more open, developmental potential of the organism, which lets it interact with its environment and change according to changing circumstances. Plastic tendencies do not fit into traditional genetic categories. We will keep this in mind as we continue.

Mendel's Experiments and the Original Concept of the Gene

Mendel's reduction proved powerful. His focus on clearly defined traits allowed a decisive experimental program.

He crossed plants, attending only to two differing traits. He crossed, for example, violet-flowered pea plants with white-flowered pea plants. The resulting hybrids had only violet flowers. When these hybrids were allowed to self-pollinate, their offspring once again had violet and white flowers, but there were more of the former than of the latter. Because crosses always resulted in more violet than white flowers, Mendel spoke of violet as a "dominant" and of white as a "recessive" trait.

Mendel and his assistants now began tediously counting the exact number of violet-flowered and white-flowered plants. In one experiment, for example, they recorded 705 violet-flowered plants and 224 white-flowered plants. Mendel had studied mathematics and physics, and he noticed that the numbers found in this second hybrid generation always expressed a numerical relationship of approximately three to one (in the above case, 3.15 to 1). With this ratio clearly before his mind's eye, Mendel was able to explain his results.[1]

It was a riddle for Mendel, as it is for anyone who thinks about the experimental results, that all the plants of the first hybrid generation show only one of the two original traits, whereas both reappear in the following generation. It seems logical to suppose, as Mendel did, that "something" responsible for white flowers must be present even in the violet-flowered first hybrid generation; otherwise,

---

1.   Interestingly, Charles Darwin performed experiments with plant hybrids at about this same time. He obtained similar results and, like Mendel, counted the instances of each type of trait in the second hybrid generation. But he went no further; he did not "see" any numerical relationships. Darwin had a powerful intellect, but it was Mendel who inaugurated the mathematical penetration of biological phenomena (Krumbiegel, 1967, p. 107).

white could not appear again in the following generation. A trait cannot simply arise out of nothing.

This thought implies that all other traits also have a "something" that stands behind them, explaining their appearance. These "somethings" Mendel called "elements," "factors," or (in German) *Anlagen* of heredity; he had no set terminology. But the concept pro forma is set: it is the concept of the gene in its original form. (The term "gene" was not coined until 1909, as we shall see; for now I will use "factor" in describing Mendel's work.) The factor is conceived as a clearly defined unit, like the trait it represents. It is, in addition, presumed to be constantly present in the background, unlike the transient coming and going of the traits.

Mendel constructed schemes (Table 1) symbolizing the hereditary factors with letters. By positing a realm of factors behind the traits, he was able to proceed with sharp-edged thoughts even though the phenomena themselves were not so stark. In particular, he could form a clear picture about how the numerical relationships came about.

Table 1: Mendelian Crossing Scheme.

Scheme to clarify the results of Mendel's crossing experiments. x = *cross;* A = *factor for dominant trait;* a = *factor for recessive trait.*

	GENES
Cross of parental generation:	AA x aa
Separation of factors in germ cells :	A A a a
Factor combinations in first hybrid generation:	Aa Aa Aa Aa
Cross of first hybrid generation :	Aa x Aa
Separation of factors in germ cells:	A A a a
Factor combinations in second hybrid generation :	AA Aa Aa aa

The results of the hybridization experiments can thus be explained in Mendelian terms as follows: Violet-flowered plants (containing only the dominant factor "A") are crossed with white-flowered plants (containing only the recessive factor "a"). All their offspring have both factors ("Aa"). Since the factor for violet (A) dominates the factor for white (a), violet appears in all plants. Mendel postulated that when these first-generation, hybrid plants are crossed, or allowed to self-pollinate, then the two "opposing" (*widerstrebende*) factors separate, each going into a different germ cell. If the germ cells then fuse in a random manner—another theoretical demand—all possible combinations of genes will be present in the next generation of hybrids. According to the scheme, three quarters of the plants of the second hybrid generation will have violet flowers (AA, Aa, Aa) and only one quarter will have white flowers (aa). And this is what Mendel found.

The Mendelian laws of heredity are based on these experiments with peas. But Mendel experimented with other plants as well. In some cases he found similar results, but others did not conform to what we in retrospect regard as *the* Mendelian scheme of heredity.

In experiments with beans, Mendel noticed that color did not follow the pattern he had found in peas, although the form traits did (Mendel, 1866). For example, he crossed red and white flowering beans. Instead of red-flowering first-generation hybrids, he found various color gradations ranging from red to pale violet.

The results of experiments with hawkweed (a member of the Composite family, like the dandelion) were, as Mendel put it, the opposite of what he had found in peas (Mendel, 1870). The second and third generation of hybrids continued to resemble the first generation hybrids. There was no separation into the original parental traits. Little did Mendel know that in hawkweed he had chosen to work with one of those not-so-rare weeds, like dandelion or groundsel, that can produce seeds without any fertilization at all.

Understandably, Mendel's fame stems from those experiments that allowed the greatest intellectual penetration. The others showed that heredity—even if one does not take the environment into account—is not so straightforward; but these nonconforming results receded into the background as genetics took the path that led to the clearest interpretation.

Hereditary Factors and Object-Thinking

A pea plant develops out of a colorless germ, taking on color and form in the course of development. In germinating, the seed gives up its form, its color fades, and it gradually decomposes. Meanwhile the seedling is growing. The roots penetrate the soil and the green leaves unfold off the elongating and branching stem. Out of the green buds the white or violet flowers emerge. After a few days the individual flowers begin to wilt and discolor.

The traits "yellow seed" or "violet flower" represent one part of this process. They are abstracted from the whole and held fast as isolated, static concepts. Our mental hold upon the Mendelian trait is worth comparing with the awareness of plant form we tried to develop in chapter 1. In attempting to grasp a dandelion as a dandelion or a poppy as a poppy, we began with the individual leaf forms. We then imaginatively transformed one leaf into the next, bridging the gap between the separate forms, and so discovering the unity of the entire series—and even of the multiple series found in successive environments.

There was no single leaf nor any other material exemplar to which we could point and say, "*That* is the species character."

Thus there are two different ways we can think about the perceived particulars. The one we explored in chapter 1 requires us to sink ourselves contemplatively into the phenomena available to observation. As we bring these phenomena into movement, we enter all the more intensively into their qualities, and the unity we finally recognize, while produced in thought, retains its strong, qualitative feel. This unity, you might say, has "dandelion" written all over it.

The other way to think about the material particulars is virtually opposite to the first. We withdraw from the qualities, letting them drop away in favor of quantity and abstraction. We count seeds and flowers. We reduce the manifold aspects of the pea plant to the simple geometrical antithesis between "round" and "angular" seeds, and to the antithesis between "violet" and "white" flowers. When we assemble a definition of the pea plant from such abstractions, we can indeed teach people to identify varieties of peas with its aid, but the definition does not have "pea" written all over it. Identification becomes less a matter of recognizing the whole plant than of collecting a set of discrete, relatively abstract characteristics.

It does not really matter to the Mendelian approach whether the flower color is red, violet, yellow, or white. What matters is that there are two clearly distinguishable color variations whose instances can be counted. Flower color as a quality of the pea plant as a whole can be ignored.

There is another difference between the two methods. The qualitative penetration of a plant's nature requires intense inner exertion. Our thinking must become active and muscular, shaping itself to the plant—but to aspects of the plant not wholly given to our senses. On the other hand, when opting for abstraction and quantity, we must be very rigorous in carrying through the intended experimental program. We focus on counting, on crossing only those plants that are supposed to be crossed, on keeping accurate records over years, and so on. Here we attend less to the plant than to our own experimental activity and the particular results it fosters.

Mendelian factors are one step further removed than traits from the full, qualitative life of the plant. They carry even less of the pea's signature. Factors are thought constructs standing "behind" the phenomena. Mendel conceived of the factors to explain to himself the results of his experiments. He left the richness of the plant itself—a richness he knew well—in favor of finding an explanatory principle.

The intellect seeks explanations. It brings light by allowing us to separate the muddled things of the world and the mind into clearly defined categories. Applying this power in Mendelian genetics, I separate out aspects of the plant as a whole and attend to individual traits. I mentally hold onto these traits, following them through years of experiments, counting and finding regularities. Then I insert a realm of discrete, separating-and-combining factors behind the traits.

In the heredity scheme of the factors (Table 1) I can follow in my mind a process that is completely clear. This scheme concurs with the experimental results, giving me a sense of understanding. What I have understood is my own thought process and its correspondence to the reduced sector of phenomena I am concerned with.

Mendel offered no physical interpretation of factors. He knew they were abstractions—that is, thought constructs—placed behind the phenomena to illuminate them. Nonetheless, he implied that factors must exist "in" the plant; otherwise he would not have spoken of factors separating from each other in the process of germ cell formation. Implicitly, Mendel began to reify the factor.

And when we look more closely, we discover that by its very nature the concept of the factor or the gene tends toward embodiment or reification. Mendel conceived factors in the mode of inanimate objects. Like solid bodies, they mutually exclude each other; they do not interpenetrate. They are discrete entities that persist. The inherent process of transformation that we have come to know in the plant is lacking. Change in the realm of factors means new combinations, not transformation.

It is a small step from a factor conceived in such object terms to the search for the factor itself as a perceptible object. We will follow this embodiment in the next chapter.

CHAPTER THREE

Genes and Knowledge

Where Are the Genes?

In 1866, the year in which Mendel's article was published, the renowned biologist Ernst Haeckel speculated that the nucleus of the cell is responsible for the inheritance of characteristics, while the surrounding cell plasma is responsible for adaptation to outer conditions (Haeckel, 1866, p. 288). Little was known at that time about the cell nucleus and cell plasma, so Haeckel had almost no empirical evidence for his claim. It was just a hunch about where two significant aspects of life—heredity and adaptation—might be embodied in the organism.

The cell nucleus was discovered in the 1830s. (In the following description I draw from Portugal and Cohen, 1978, chapters 2 and 6.) In 1842 Karl Naegli, a biologist with whom Mendel later corresponded, observed that the cell nucleus does not always appear as a homogeneous mass; its contents occasionally congeal into little rod-shaped bodies. Later, with better staining techniques, this congealing was observed to occur during cell division. In

1884 the rod-shaped bodies were named "chromosomes" (from the Greek, meaning "colored bodies").

The late nineteenth century brought many new observations concerning the chromosomes and their role in cell division. The number of chromosomes per cell in a given organism appeared to be constant. There were an even number of chromosomes, and they had characteristic shapes and sizes that were recognizably the same in every cell (figure 15).

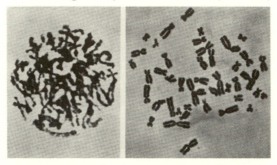

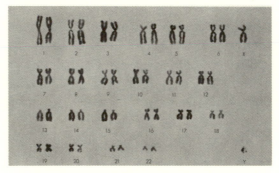

FIGURE 15. Chromosomes from a human white blood cell. Human white blood cells were treated with a colchicine derivative to arrest cell division at the stage when the chromosomes are most visible (top left). The cells were then treated with a salt solution, causing them to swell and the chromosomes to separate; only then do the distinct structures in the picture on the top right appear. Now the chromosomes in each cell can be counted and measured. The picture at the bottom shows the chromosomes from one cell ordered in homologous pairs (from Bearn and German, 1961).

Mature germ cells—eggs and sperm—were a little different. They had only half as many chromosomes as other cells. But this made sense because, also unlike other cells, germ cells combine in producing the next generation. When fertilization occurs, the nuclei of sperm and egg fuse to become a single, new nucleus. If these germ cells each have six chromosomes, then the nucleus of the fertilized egg has twelve. So the number of chromosomes remains constant in each new generation of a species.

What does all this have to do with heredity? At first glance, not much. But eggs and sperm are the only cells—and therefore the only material—to pass from one generation to the next. They are the physical bridge between generations. So the more we know about these cells, the more we might learn about heredity.

But no one in the nineteenth century connected these cytological observations with Mendel's work. This is one of those historical riddles showing that science does not progress in a straightforward manner.

When Mendel died in 1884, his work was essentially unknown. (By contrast, Charles Darwin's *Origin of Species* sold out shortly after its arrival on the bookshelves.) Mendel's paper appeared in a journal with a small circle of readers. The few scientists with whom Mendel corresponded about his work and the few authors who cited his paper seemed not to have grasped its implications. Why didn't Naegli, who knew both about the cell and about Mendel's work, see any connections? In any case, the mathematical approach to biological phenomena was new, and Mendel's paper was not easy reading. The time was not ripe.

The situation changed drastically at the outset of the twentieth century. In 1900, within the course of a few months, three botanists—Hugo de Vries, Carl Correns, and Erich von Tschermak—published articles on heredity. Each worked independently and performed experiments similar to Mendel's. Their results supported Mendel's findings, and they cited Mendel's work in their articles. Mendel finally became a name in biology.

The Chromosome Theory of Heredity

Now, put yourself in the shoes of a Columbia University graduate student, William Sutton, in the first years of this century. Steeped in the results of Mendelian experiments, you are researching chromosomes in a particular species of grasshopper. Under your microscope you see twenty-two chromosomes in an immature germ cell. During cell division the chromosomes line up in eleven pairs. The members of each pair are identical in appearance, and are therefore called "homologous pairs."

You then find that the pairs have separated, with each mature germ cell containing eleven chromosomes. This proves to be the case for egg cells as well as sperm cells. After egg and sperm fuse during fertilization, twenty-two chromosomes reappear. They look just the same as the twenty-two chromosomes in the cells of the parents, but they represent a new combination, since eleven have come from the male parent and eleven from the female parent.

If you are looking at the chromosomes with the eyes and mind of William Sutton, you see them as an embodiment of Mendelian hereditary factors:

- Mendel conceived of the factors as discrete entities. Correspondingly, the nucleus divides into separate chromosomes.

- Mendel hypothesized pairs of factors (in our previous terminology, AA or Aa or aa). Chromosomes appear in homologous, or identical, pairs.

- The pairs of factors in the Mendelian scheme separate. In germ-cell division the homologous pairs separate.

- In a crossing scheme, the factors from the parents are paired again. In fertilization, new homologous pairs are formed.

- The number of factors remains the same and the factors themselves don't change. Likewise, there are a constant number of chromosomes in each cell and each generation, and their shape and size remain the same.

Sutton concluded: "Thus the phenomena of germ cell division and of heredity are seen to have the same essential features, viz., purity of units (chromosomes, characters) and the independent transmission of the same" (Sutton, 1903). What a wonderful correspondence between things and thought constructs—between chromosomes and Mendelian factors "behind" the phenomena!

How did Sutton interpret this correlation? He writes, "chromosome A from the father and its homologue, chromosome a, from the mother...may be regarded as the physical bases of the antagonistic unit-characters [factors] A and a of father and mother." In other words, the chromosomes carry or contain the factors. This is the chromosome theory of heredity. Because the chromosomes separate, the factors separate; because chromosomes from the parents come together in fertilization, new combinations of factors arise in the offspring. Mendel's results and his interpretation with factors can now be explained by the chromosome theory of heredity.

In the first decade of the twentieth century, scientists used a variety of terms—for example, "unit character" or "determinant"—to designate the mendelian hereditary factors. This variety was confusing, and in 1909, the biologist W. Johannsen suggested the term *gene*. Its use became prevalent. Johannsen defined the concept of the gene broadly, with no reference to the chromosomes, showing that the chromosome theory had not yet become generally accepted:

> The word *gene* is completely free of any hypothesis; it expresses only the evident fact that, in any case, many characteristics of the organism are specified in the germ cells by means of special conditions, foundations, and determiners which are present in unique, separate, and thereby independent ways—in short, precisely what we wish to call genes. (Quoted in Portugal and Cohen, 1978, p. 118)

From here on, I will use the word *gene*.

The chromosome theory found increasing confirmation in the following decades. Especially important was the work of T. H. Morgan's research group at Columbia University. In their "fly room" they bred many thousands of fruit flies (the small flies you have seen around rotting fruit). Every once in a while they observed a fly with a unique hereditary trait—white eyes instead of the typical red eyes, veinless wings instead of the normal veined wings. Animals having such traits were called mutants. Morgan's group bred mutant flies with normal flies, just as Mendel bred different varieties of peas. By 1922 they had identified two thousand mutant traits and deduced the presence of two thousand different genes.

The chromosome theory suggests that all these genes must be connected to the fly's chromosomes. But the fruit fly has only four pairs of chromosomes, implying that there must be many genes on or in a chromosome. The hereditary consequence is that those genes ought to be inherited as a group.

And this is exactly what the breeding experiments suggested. Morgan's group found, for example, that black body, reduced body hair and vestigial (very small) wings are linked together. Sepia eye color, curled wings, and stubbled body hair are part of a different "linkage group," the term coined for traits that are inherited together.

If two genes (for example, AA) stand behind any given trait and if these two genes are associated with the two chromosomes of one homologous pair, then there should be, according to the chromosome theory, exactly as many groups of linked traits as there are pairs of homologous chromosomes. The fruit fly has four homologous pairs. How many linkage groups did Morgan's group find? Precisely four! In addition, the smallest linkage group was correlated with the smallest pair of chromosomes.

A theory is all the more convincing as it deals successfully with phenomena that apparently falsify it. Morgan's group found that linked traits were not *always* linked (Sturtevant and Beadle, 1962, chapter 6). In 2.5% of the cases black body and reduced hair were not linked, and in 9.5% of the cases black body was not linked with vestigial wings. But instead of dropping the chromosome theory, the researchers ingeniously extended it. They hypothesized that genes were being exchanged between chromosomes (so-called *crossing-over*). What they subsequently found in cells was, in fact, that homologous pairs intertwined before they separated. Couldn't they exchange genes during this embrace?

Morgan's group used the initially discomforting idea of crossing-over as a springboard for more far-reaching considerations. Two genes far apart on a chromosome would more likely be separated by random crossing-over than two neighboring genes. (If ten people form a chain holding hands and the chain is broken, then the two people on the ends will always be separated, while the probability that the chain will break between any particular pair of people standing next to each other is much smaller.)

So the frequency of crossing-over should indicate the relative distance between genes on a chromosome. According to the frequency of crossing-over, the gene for black body would be nearer to the gene for reduced hair (2.5% linkage failure) than it would be to the gene for vestigial wings (9.5% failure). Following this principle, researchers constructed the first linear map showing the order of genes on chromosomes in 1913.

Later it became possible to observe how structural changes in the chromosomes correlated with changes in linkage groups. By the 1930s most scientists were convinced that the chromosomes were the home of genes.

Genes and DNA

The chromosome theory gives the genes a place in the physical world. But this is not enough. In their textbook from 1939, Sturtevant and Beadle, two foremost geneticists of the time, explain in great detail the chromosome theory and its confirmation through experiment. At the end of the book they find it "pertinent to inquire into the nature of the gene" (p. 335). Despite all the advances, the question remains, What are the genes?

While genes have been located in the chromosomes, they are not yet bodies. They do not have a "thing-nature." They are still thought constructs. But they are nonetheless powerful. Sturtevant and Beadle conclude:

> In a specified environment, genes determine what kind of an individual a representative of a given species is going to be. There can be little doubt that genes also determine to what species a given individual will belong. By logical extension, it can be argued that genes determine whether an organism is a plant or an animal, as well as what kind of a plant or animal. And, to carry these deductions still further, genes determine whether or not an organism is going to develop at all. (p. 334)

Geneticists in 1939 knew that genes exist, they knew what they determine, and they knew that they are part of the chromosomes. But about their material nature, "there is little in the way to go on, and one is forced to resort to speculation" (p. 335).

What Is the Substance of Genes?

The path of embodiment demanded that genes be substances. If the substance of genes could be found, then one could finally say that genes are the material causes of traits. But the results of breeding experiments and microscopic observations do not yield substances. Substance is the domain of biochemistry. Biochemical investigations needed to be added to the edifice of genetics.

Biochemists knew before 1940 that chromosomes could be analyzed into proteins and nucleic acids. There was a good deal of discussion about whether proteins or nucleic acids are the substance of genes.

The experiments of Oswald Avery and co-workers finally gave a clear answer to the question (Avery et al., 1944). They worked with two types (strains) of the same species of bacteria that inhabit lung tissue. One strain formed smooth, glistening colonies; it was called the S-strain (S for smooth). The other strain formed rough colonies and was called the R-strain. S-strain bacteria are related to the occurrence of pneumonia; R-strain bacteria are not.

Avery and his co-workers killed and chemically analyzed S-strain bacteria. They then added an extract from this analysis to a growing culture of R-strain bacteria. Under certain conditions some R-strain bacteria were subsequently transformed into S-strain bacteria. This change, moreover, was hereditary. In genetic terms: R-strain had taken on a new trait—forming smooth colonies. The extract from the S-strain must have been genetic material that caused the R-strain bacteria to manifest this new trait.

What was this extract from the S-strain? Pure deoxyribonucleic acid—DNA. When Avery and his co-workers added an enzyme known to break down DNA, the experiment did not work. Only DNA had the transformative effect. They had found the substance of the genes.

DNA and the Central Dogma

After this discovery, scientific interest in the structure of DNA quickened. In 1953 Watson and Crick unveiled their now famous double-helix model of DNA. Their model plausibly explained how DNA might function as the genetic material. They discovered no new facts, but put existing facts and models together into a convincing and comprehensive picture. This picture was a great catalyst for genetics, more or less initiating the era of molecular biology. Progress was thus furthered by an idea that can be pictured as an object, even down to the form of a stick-and-ball physical model.

In 1958 Crick formulated the "Central Dogma of Molecular Biology." It presents a rigid mechanism, and also reveals, as Crick put it later, "a boundless optimism that the basic concepts involved were rather simple and probably much the same in all living things" (Crick, 1970). The Central Dogma describes a mechanism by which genes could determine traits via protein synthesis and expression of the so-called genetic code. "Genetic information," according to this dogma, flows only from the genes to the proteins, and not vice versa.

Why are traits associated with proteins? There are two categories of proteins. Structural proteins like keratin are found in hair, fingernails, and cornified skin; they can, therefore, show up as part of many traits. Then there are functional proteins, called enzymes. Enzymes catalyze all physiological reactions in organisms, so that they are absolutely essential to life. Each enzyme catalyzes a specific reaction.

We can analyze, for example, how the skin darkens when someone gets a sun tan. In the lower layer of the upper skin one finds the pigment called melanin. When the skin darkens, cells called melanocytes increase production of melanin. For melanocytes to produce melanin, enzymes are necessary. One of these enzymes is called tyrosinase. Tyrosinase, like other proteins, is synthesized on little organelles in the cell plasma called ribosomes. This synthesis is dependent on another type of substance—ribonucleic acid (RNA). There are different types of RNA, only one of which I mention here—messenger RNA (m-RNA). M-RNA originates in the cell nucleus, and its synthesis is dependent upon DNA.

So a chain of connecting links between DNA and a trait (skin pigmentation) is complete: skin pigmentation depends on melanin, melanin formation depends on tyrosinase, tyrosinase synthesis depends on RNA, RNA synthesis depends on DNA. Or, in reverse order, schematically:

$$DNA \rightarrow RNA \rightarrow protein\ (enzyme) \rightarrow trait$$

In the 1950s and 1960s geneticists elucidated a beautifully simple picture of how the structure of DNA could determine the structure of proteins, mediated by RNA. DNA is pictured as a linear molecule made up of repeating elements, called nucleotides. Chemical analysis of a nucleotide results in three substances: sugar, phosphate, and a nitrogenous base. While the sugar and the phosphate are the same in each nucleotide, there are four different nitrogenous bases (Adenine, Thymine, Guanine, and Cytosine). Each nucleotide contains a different base and is symbolized by the first letter of the base it contains: A, T, G, and C. If there were only one base, then DNA would be one long, uniform molecule made up of identical nucleotides. Because there are four bases, there is a sequence of nucleotides (for example, C-C-A-T-G-G-A...). Segments of DNA are distinct from one another by virtue of their base sequences.

Every gene is composed of a particular number and sequence of nucleotides. A gene's "message" is contained in its nucleotide sequence. A specific segment of DNA—a gene—serves as a template for the synthesis of m-RNA. M-RNA moves into the cell plasma, and the sequence of its nucleotides determines the sequence of amino acids in a protein (or part of a protein called a polypeptide).

The structure and function of a protein are dependent upon its amino acid sequence. There are a total of twenty different amino acids in proteins. Any given protein consists of a portion of those; the amino acids form a chain that is folded in a complicated manner.

How could the sequence of four different bases in DNA determine the sequence of twenty different amino acids in a protein? This was the "coding problem" (Crick) of the 1960s. We can look at the coding problem as a problem of mathematical permutations. Four single units are given in the four different nucleotides: A, T, C, and G. If we link two of these units together, and assume that pairs like AT and TA are distinct by virtue of their order, then we end up with sixteen different pairs of nucleotides (AA AT AC AG; TA TT TC TG; CA CT CC CG; GA GT GC GG). These sixteen different code words are not enough, since we need one code word for each of the twenty different amino acids. We can add one more nucleotide to each of the sixteen pairs. For example, adding to the first pair, AA, results in four groups of three nucleotides: AAA, AAT, AAC, AAG. If we do the same with every other pair, we arrive at a total of 64 (16 x 4) different groups of three nucleotides. This is a much larger number than needed, but in any case, one or more groups of three nucleotides could form the code words—now called *codons*—for each amino acid.

And, indeed, this idea was supported by experimental evidence. By 1969 it was clear which groups of three nucleotides stood for which amino acids. One could deduce the nucleotide sequence of a gene by knowing the sequence of amino acids in a protein (or polypeptide). The genetic code had been deciphered; it was clear how the structure of DNA determined the structure of proteins.[1]

---

1. I have given only a skeletal picture of the relation between genes, proteins, and traits. The reader can turn to any biology textbook for more information. For a detailed but very readable historical account, see Judson, 1979. The classic genetics textbook is Watson's *Molecular Biology of the Gene*, 1987.

The crystal clear and simple mechanism was convincing, and stimulated an enormous amount of research. Many experimental results could be interpreted as supporting the theory, and in the 1960s the high point of a one-dimensional, mechanistic view of heredity was reached. Many textbook descriptions still largely follow this original picture. It also sustains the everyday "knowledge" in our time that DNA is the primary substance of heredity, encoding all the information required to determine an organism's characteristics.

Complications

Already in the 1960s some scientists criticized a simple, one-dimensional view of inheritance. Barry Commoner, for example, emphasized the fact that each step in the synthesis of DNA, RNA, or protein involves specific enzymes as catalyzers. Enzymes are clearly the result of a process of synthesis, but they are also absolutely necessary functional components in building up or breaking down substances, including DNA and RNA.

> Thus transmission of biochemical specificity within the cell is fundamentally circular rather than linear and the total system rather than any single constituent is responsible for the biochemical specificity which gives rise to biological specificity.... Biochemical specificity embodied in DNA nucleotide sequence arises partly in pre-existing DNA and partly in pre-existing proteins. At the same time, biochemical specificity embodied in the amino-acid sequence of protein arises partly in protein and partly in DNA. In effect, this is the familiar "chicken and egg" relationship of biology expressed on a molecular level. (Commoner, 1968)

In the 1970s and the 1980s further oversimplifications associated with the Central Dogma became evident. Genes and heredity proved more complex and less rigid than researchers had imagined. Apparent anomalies had been discovered many years earlier, but they were difficult to understand and did not fit into any existing, simple schemes. They tended to be ignored. I will mention only a few examples.

You will recall that Morgan and his co-workers posited the crossing-over, or exchange, of genes between homologous chromosomes. Further research showed that genes did not merely switch positions; depending on the new position of a gene, its function might change as well. A gene connected to the formation of extra wing hairs showed no effects in one particular location, while the normal gene in a new position produced effects similar to those of the "hairy" gene (Sturtevant and Beadle, 1962, p. 224ff.). This is called the position effect. Evidently, genes are not as immune to their context as had been thought.

The significant but long overlooked work of Barbara McClintock with maize showed clearly the dynamic nature of genetic processes (Keller, 1983). Her breeding experiments led her to conclude that genes must be regularly moving between chromosomes. Depending on where a gene moved, it had different effects on the development of traits. Such transposable genetic elements, or "jumping genes," are now known to be ubiquitous and associated with both normal and abnormal processes. But the significance of McClintock's discoveries in the 1940s was not recognized until the 1970s. She received a Nobel Prize in 1983.

Geneticists now know that antibiotic-resistant strains of bacteria reproduce the genes connected to resistance and pass them on as transposable elements to other bacteria, which then become resistant themselves (Cohen and Shapiro, 1980; Meyer, 1983). Jumping genes were also found to be important in the development of the mammalian immune system. Researchers discovered that during fetal development segments of DNA in the chromosomes are repositioned, and only then do they become functional antibody genes (Tonegawa, 1983; Schwartz, 1995b). The rearrangement of DNA segments allows for the great number of different antibodies. Almost 10% of human genes may be jumping genes (Schwartz, 1995a).

You recall that, according to the models of the 1960s, the genetic information of a segment of DNA—a gene—is transcribed into messenger RNA that in turn is translated into a protein. Then researchers made the surprising discovery that, in the cells of higher organisms, messenger RNA is altered by enzymes before its information is translated into protein (Chambon, 1981). In the language of genetics, pieces of RNA are excised from the molecule and the remaining pieces are fused to make the functional RNA that then serves as the template for protein synthesis. There is no one-to-one correspondence between DNA sequence and proteins. Struck by the discrepancy between traditional models and these findings, Ernst Peter Fischer concludes:

There are, therefore, no genes! There are—at least in the cells of higher organisms—only pieces of genes, which the cell can use when it makes proteins. A gene is by no means a molecule that exists in the cell. Rather, a gene is a task that a cell has to accomplish. Genes don't exist; they are always becoming. (Fischer, 1991, p. 111; my translation)

Regardless of how one defines genes, simple, mono-causal, one-directional schemes as epitomized by the Central Dogma are no longer credible. Nonetheless, the ideal of finding underlying mechanisms remains. In models, the genetic machine has become dynamic, but it remains a machine. A radical rethinking of genetic categories has not occurred. And in many minds one imperative still exists: the organism shall be reduced to its genes.

DNA and Information

The well-known geneticist Walter Gilbert is of the opinion that through the Human Genome Project "half of the total knowledge of the human organism will be available in five to seven years, and all of it by the end of the decade" (Gilbert, 1991). Where is this knowledge to come from? Nowhere else but from the genes—or more precisely, from the exact structure (nucleotide sequence) of DNA in human cells. One cannot find a clearer statement of belief in the possibility of total reduction of an organism to its genes. Knowledge of genes is taken as knowledge of the organism. I do not want to imply that all geneticists hold this extreme view, but it is a prevalent one, with great suggestive power.

Let's consider this belief in light of some recent findings. From a genetic standpoint, yeast (*Saccharomyces cerevisiae*) is one of the best-known organisms. In the spring of 1992 a certain milestone in genetic research was attained with yeast: for the first time researchers determined the complete DNA sequence of a whole chromosome of an organism (Chromosome III in this case). Thirty-five different laboratories in seventeen European countries were involved in the project; the article had 147 authors (Oliver et al., 1992). Before this collaborative research, thirty-four genes had been known to be connected with Chromosome III. The complete sequencing now suggested 182 genes—that is, 148 new genes were found.

Since a gene is defined not only by the model of its molecular structure, but also by the trait(s) to which it is related, the question arises whether these newly discovered DNA sequences are really genes (that is, related to functions in the organism) or just "meaningless" pieces of DNA. The only way to determine this is to disturb the genes ("gene disruption") and observe whether any effects are noticeable. This was done with fifty-five of the new genes, and physiological changes such as hypersensitivity to various drugs, sterility, and changes in heat and cold sensitivity were observed in fourteen cases. In the other cases disruption showed no effect (which does not mean that future tests will not show an effect).

The authors conclude that "our understanding of yeast physiology and cell biology is lagging behind our molecular genetic analysis." Another way of viewing it is this: we gain a knowledge of genes—as opposed to a mere assertion of their material existence—only through knowledge of the organism as a whole. The more knowledge we have of the organism as a whole, the more information we have. *This information is not in the genes; it is the conceptual thread that weaves together the various details into a meaningful whole.*

A discovery made by the yeast researchers shows this fact clearly. They found one gene that was homologous in structure to a nitrogen-fixing gene in nitrogen-fixing bacteria. Since yeast does not fix nitrogen, it is evident that this "same" gene has to be understood differently in each organism. The primary genetic information alone gives no information about a gene's significance in the organism.

Much genetic research is done on mice, since, as mammals, they are more closely related to human beings than most other experimental animals. Mice are frequently used as models for investigating human illnesses. However, the assumption that the same gene will have the same effect in both mice and humans is often falsified by experimental results.

> Natural or artificially created mutant strains of mice are of great value in studying development and disease, but often such models reveal more differences than expected.... Mouse models for Lesch-Nyhan and Gaucher's disease have been created by gene targeting, but whereas the former seem to be asymptomatic, the latter ... die within twenty-four hours of birth, making further constructs necessary before the more common presentations in humans can be mimicked. (Davies, 1992)

Such examples are by no means isolated. Looking closer to home, retinoblastomas are tumors that form in the developing retina of children. Researchers found that a mutation in the so-called retinoblastoma gene is connected to this tumor formation. If a child carries a mutated gene from its parents, there is an 85% chance that it will develop the tumor; but mice with the same genetic condition do not. In fact, retinoblastomas do not naturally occur in mice or any other vertebrate; they are confined to humans. If, however, a mouse carries the gene from both parents, there is a devastating outcome: it dies while still in the womb. So a mutation in the same gene produces completely different consequences. Indeed, if the functional relations are so different, are we justified in calling it the same gene in both cases (Harlow, 1992)?

Geneticists who let the facts speak and are not already convinced of a particular mission for genetic research are critical of the tendency to oversimplify. Thus D. Pritchard responded to Gilbert's essay cited above: "It is a modern myth that DNA contains all the information necessary to produce that organism. This is not so" (Pritchard, 1991).

The Human Genome Project

The Human Genome Project is an international effort to determine and map all human genes, of which there are assumed to be approximately one hundred thousand. Dr. Francis Collins, the director of the National Center for Human Genome Research, calls the project "the most important and the most significant project that humankind has ever mounted" (quoted in Kolata, 1993b). The project, Collins hopes, will elucidate the causes of genetically based diseases, preparing the way for therapies.

Regarding such goals, a lesson can be learned from the research dealing with sickle cell anemia, the first disease to be termed a molecular disease (described in Stryer, 1988). In 1904 the Chicago doctor James Herrick cared for a young black student who showed an unfamiliar array of symptoms. The patient had a cough and fever, he felt weak, was often dizzy, and had headaches. In the previous year he had suffered heart palpitations. His heart was enlarged. He had signs of jaundice, with evidence of kidney damage. He was anemic, and an examination showed that the number of red blood cells was half of normal.

Then Herrick discovered something new: "The shape of the red cells was very irregular but what especially attracted attention was the large number of thin, elongated, sickle-shaped and crescent-shaped forms" (quoted in Stryer, 1988, p. 163). Herrick prescribed rest and nourishing food. The patient gradually felt better and became less anemic. His blood picture improved—there were fewer sickle-shaped red blood cells.

Although he did not name it, Herrick had discovered sickle cell anemia. Later, after more cases in black communities were diagnosed, it became clear that sickle cell anemia could be interpreted as following a Mendelian pattern of inheritance. If a child received a "sickle cell gene" from both parents, then usually he or she became ill.

What do the sickle-shaped red blood cells have to do with the illness? Red blood cells from a normal individual take on a sickle form when the concentration of oxygen is reduced. This pointed to hemoglobin, the protein isolable from red blood cells. Hemoglobin is essential for oxygen utilization. Subsequently it was found that oxygen is not nearly as soluble in sickle cell hemoglobin as it is in normal hemoglobin.

The Nobel laureate chemist Linus Pauling compared normal and sickle cell hemoglobin from a chemical and physical point of view. He found differences that he concluded resulted from some unknown change in one gene. He coined the term *molecular disease* in 1949.

The hemoglobin protein can be analyzed into 574 amino acids. In 1954 the biochemist Vernon Ingram discovered that, in relation to normal hemoglobin, only one amino acid is different in sickle cell hemoglobin. On the basis of the genetic code, one could conclude in the 1960s that the DNA forming the gene for hemoglobin is also changed only at one particular point. The connection between trait (sickle cell anemia) and DNA had been made.

Later, in 1989, Luzzatto and Goodfellow wrote a short summary of the present state of sickle cell anemia research

and therapy, entitled "A simple disease with no cure." The
following is an excerpt:

> Molecular biology explained the basic defect in sickle
> cell anemia and has provided the tools for prenatal
> diagnosis, but the treatment of afflicted patients under-
> going crisis has not correspondingly improved....
> Although all patients with sickle cell anemia have
> exactly the same genetic defect, there is wide variation
> in clinical expression of the disease.... Sickle cell ane-
> mia has always been paradigmatic for molecular analy-
> sis of genetic disease and the disappointing progress in
> treating it could be a warning for those studying other
> diseases. As is clear from the example of sickle cell ane-
> mia, avoidance of this fate will require continued stud-
> ies on the natural history of diseases and the
> physiological interactions in the whole organism: per-
> haps a true anti-sickling agent will then turn up.

Lander and Schork add:

> Even the simplest disease is complex, when looked at
> closely. Sickle cell anemia is a classic example.... Indi-
> viduals carrying identical [genes] can show markedly
> different clinical courses, varying from early childhood
> mortality to a virtually unrecognized condition at the
> age of fifty. (Lander and Schork, 1994)

Molecular information, knowledge of the disease in the
context of the whole individual, and the ability to treat
patients are quite different things. Herrick's patient in
1904 would not be better off as a result of the molecular
knowledge of 1995. I do not mean to criticize the struggles
for a better understanding of this disease, but I *would* like

to help deflate the hot-air balloon of euphoria that often accompanies discussions of the Human Genome Project.

Along with their hopes for new therapies, project proponents claim that genetic information can be employed diagnostically to identify genetic predispositions. But what is the measuring stick for normalcy? "The trouble with this argument is that there simply is no such entity as a 'representative sequence' of the human (or any) genome; the amount of variability without the loss of function in the DNA sequence of any natural population is far too great" (Sarkar and Tauber, 1991).

Four hundred fifty variants of hemoglobin have been discovered, and almost half of them show no adverse physiological effects. Such "variants" are hence "normal." "If accurate medical diagnosis is the purpose of the use of sequence diagnosis, each arbitrary sequence will have to be independently judged for functionality" (ibid.).

Another case in point is the "cystic fibrosis gene," discovered in 1989. As often happens, euphoria greeted the discovery of the alleged cause of the disease. Since then the picture has become more and more complex. The "healthy" gene does not just mutate (change) in one place, but 350 different mutations have been found. These are partially correlated with different symptoms. Some healthy individuals, for example, can have mutations that are identical to those usually found in people with cystic fibrosis. If one considered merely their genes, then, as the researcher Barbara Handelin states, "they should have cystic fibrosis, but they clearly don't" (quoted in Kolata, 1993a).

I could cite many more cases illustrating the difficulty of relating changes in DNA to "normalcy" or illness. (For numerous instructive examples, see Hubbard and Wald, 1993.) In sum, we see that any hope of finding *the* answer in DNA is illusory. The information supposedly in DNA is only elevated to actual knowledge when DNA is seen in light of its context in the particular organism.

Mere knowledge of gene sequences will bring little benefit. As the geneticist J. S. Jones puts it:

> The world's most boring book will be the complete sequence of the human genome: three-thousand-million letters long, with no discernible plot, thousands of repeats of the same sentence, page after page of meaningless rambling, and an occasional nugget of sense— usually signifying nothing in particular.... The gene sequencers are pursuing the ultimate reductionistic program: to understand the message, we just have to put all the letters in order. There is an opposing view which suggests that, having sequenced the genome we may be in the position of a non-musician faced with the score of Wagner's Ring cycle: information, apparently making no sense at all, but in fact containing an amazing tale—if we only knew what it meant. (Jones, 1991)

In the geneticist Weissmann's statement (1983) that we as human beings can come to know ourselves through an inventory of our genes and their action, we have the reductionist version of the Greek dictum, "Man, know thyself." His statement has tremendous suggestive power, but is nonetheless based on an illusion.

The Phantom of Total Reduction

The approach of object-thinking to heredity has proven eminently successful. Again and again physical correlates of previously constructed conceptual schemes have been discovered—a process that will no doubt continue. Yet it has become clear in the course of this chapter that there is a discrepancy between claims and findings.

This is partly owing to unawareness of the consequences of reductionism as a method. Recapitulating:

We observe organisms in all their transformations and all their environmental plasticity. Then, instead of working to grasp in thought the unity of these manifestations—say, the "pea character" of the pea—we select a particular trait, such as the roundness or angularity of a seed at one stage in the life of the plant. Having carefully identified such a reliable trait, abstracted it from the environment, and frozen it in time, we now conceive of heredity factors—genes—behind the trait. The conceptual scheme helps us find order in the hereditary pattern of traits.

We then assume that the genes have some sort of physical embodiment. And, indeed, we find the chromosomes. The correlation between Mendelian genes and chromosomes is striking, but it hinges on simplification. We don't, for example, attend to the chromosomes' changing form, arising out of the undifferentiated mass of the cell nucleus. Just like the traits in the organism as a whole, the visible chromosomes come and go in the life of the cell—they are fleeting phenomena. But we ignore this fact and focus on a certain constancy in shape, size, and number. Only then does the correlation between trait and chromosome become evident.

Now the genes are in the chromosomes. But what are they? We find DNA, the material basis of the genes. But as we have done with the traits and the chromosomes, we focus on DNA in its structural aspect. Only then can we arrive at an explanatory model. A telling example: x-ray crystallography pictures are essential for building the double-helix model of DNA. To obtain such pictures, we must put DNA into crystalline form. Can the sharp-edged thoughts of the inquiring intellect find a better correlate than crystals? But DNA is not crystallized in the watery environment of the living cell; it is continually being built up and broken down as cells divide, grow, and die.

So we view the phenomena—traits, chromosomes, or DNA—as clearly defined objects. This makes them susceptible to the analysis of object-thinking. We leave out the processes of transformation that fluid thinking would take hold of.

Furthermore, we change levels of analysis, thereby losing context. We move from the living organism in its environment to the organism as a conglomerate of traits. We can then view the organs within the organism, the tissues within the organs, and the cells within the tissues. We arrive at the cell and focus on the phase in the life of the cell nucleus producing the chromosomes. We then look at the various substances in the chromosomes and focus on DNA. Every time we fix our gaze on a particular feature, we lose the context of the whole in which it is embedded.

This is an extremely effective way to gain limited, yet very exact knowledge. But we must be aware of the limitations. At each step of the reduction and analysis we leave a realm of potential knowledge behind. When we then summarize our knowledge, drawing a line all the way from DNA to traits, we have pictured the organism from only one point of view. Much has been left out along the way.

But there is more. Reductionism as an explanatory principle goes beyond reductionism as a pragmatic method. It seeks material causes. What happens when we elevate parts to causes of the whole? What are we doing when we claim that genes cause traits? *We are projecting a whole process of knowledge into a substance.* We reify our conceptual understanding. Only then can we say something like, "all the hereditary information necessary for the development of an organism is contained in DNA." But it is not true.

Alfred North Whitehead noticed the tendency within philosophy and science to reify knowledge. He called it the *fallacy of misplaced concreteness* (Whitehead, 1967, especially chapters 3 and 4). With this phrase he underscores the need to distinguish between our theories and models on the one hand, and the phenomena with which these abstractions are concerned, on the other. They are not the same. When we speak of genes, we inevitably refer to a whole set of thought-impregnated phenomena. This fact is overlooked when we reify the concept of the gene into DNA as a cause. Misplaced concreteness is inherent in reductionist object-thinking.

Consider what it means to know or understand something. I observe the thing, and it appears as a riddle to my mind; I do not fully understand what I have observed. I ask questions, and with questioning my thinking about my observations begins. I make more observations and ponder the connections between them. Suddenly or gradually, I come to feel I have understood something when concepts illuminate my perceptions, placing them in a coherent and meaningful context. I gain understanding. Knowing thus involves uniting (without mixing up) the perceptual and the conceptual (Steiner, 1986).

When scientists try to find answers to questions that, while raised by their own thinking, are imagined to lie *beyond* thought—that is, in pure materiality—then their undertaking becomes futile, for science always involves penetrating and ordering experience with thought. Every scientist knows this, and yet, the search for underlying material causes remains an ideal.

Instead of trying to find connections *between* the phenomena, object-thinking seeks causes *behind* them. Scientists construct object-like models, but because the models are not yet real objects—because they are "only" thoughts—their object-thinking seeks to fill the models with matter. This filling is attempted through the discovery of new phenomena, for which new models are formed, because without thoughts there can be no explanations. But then a material correlate is again sought. And so the cycle repeats. We cannot transcend thought to reach some imagined state of the purely material.

By continually abandoning the phenomena that are given to us, and by translating explanations into causal objects pictured behind the phenomena, we give up the possibility of gaining satisfactory understanding. We embark instead upon an infinite regress in which the actual, full-bodied phenomena are continuously being lost.

When the nature of object-thinking is not understood, then illusions and inflated claims arise. There is no fundamental cause, no "atom" of genetics. *The* material cause to which everything can be reduced is a phantom.

But genetic pictures of life do not hover uselessly above the world, only affecting the minds of scientists. The pictures flow into the hands and instruments that change the world. Genetics is also a doing, a creating through experiment and technology. We turn to this aspect in the next chapter.

CHAPTER FOUR

Thought and Deed in Experimentation

Involvement

When scientists perform experiments, it is usually to test a hunch or a thought, called a hypothesis. They do not simply proclaim an idea's truth, nor do they restrict themselves to passive observation of naturally occurring phenomena. Instead they actively pursue a dialogue with nature called the experimental method.

Researchers create conditions under which they can test a guiding thought. The thought shapes the experiment. But the experiment also depends upon the scientist's skill in arranging adequate conditions. Thought and action come together creatively, so that new dimensions of a phenomenon can reveal themselves. The revelation is impossible without both elements.

Mendel's pea plants, left to themselves, would normally self-pollinate, but to test his ideas Mendel had to cross-pollinate them. To this end he took flowers in the bud stage and carefully removed each of the ten stamens in every flower. This prohibited self-pollination and allowed him to pollinate each flower with pollen from a different pea plant. He opened a flower, gathered its pollen with a fine brush, went to another (destaminated) flower, opened it, and placed the pollen on the flower's pistil.

We see here how actions help to realize a particular thought—in this case, a thought about how traits are inherited in pea hybrids. Such a realization involves planning, self-control, careful manipulation, and an exact record of one's steps. (A single mislabeled plant or flask can have devastating consequences, leading to false conclusions or to an explosion.)

Looked at in this way, the experiment is a dynamic process mediating one's understanding of the world. The scientist is actively engaged as a knower and a doer. Discovery of new aspects of the phenomena under investigation is at the same time a training and an extension of cognitive faculties.

The dangers of experimentation are not just physical. Two hundred years ago Goethe masterfully described the "inner enemies" of the experimenter in his essay, "The Experiment as Mediator between Object and Subject":

> Thus we can never be too careful in our efforts to avoid drawing hasty conclusions from experiments or using them directly as proof to bear out some theory. For here at this pass, this transition from empirical evidence to judgment, cognition to application, all the inner enemies of man lie in wait: imagination, which sweeps him away on its wings before he knows his feet have left the ground; impatience; haste; self-satisfaction; rigidity; formalistic thought; prejudice; ease; frivolity; fickleness—this whole throng and its retinue.

Here they lie in ambush and surprise not only the active observer but also the contemplative one who appears safe from all passion....

I would venture to say that we cannot prove anything by one experiment or even several experiments together, that nothing is more dangerous than the desire to prove some thesis directly through experiments, that the greatest errors have arisen just where the dangers and shortcomings in this method have been overlooked....

Every piece of empirical evidence, every experiment, must be viewed as isolated, yet the human faculty of thought forcibly strives to unite all external objects known to it. It is easy to see the risk we run when we try to connect a single bit of evidence with an idea already formed, or use individual experiments to prove some relationship not fully perceptible to the senses but expressed through the creative power of the mind....

Such efforts generally give rise to theories and systems which are a tribute to their author's intelligence. But with undue applause or protracted support they soon begin to hinder and harm the very progress of the human mind they had earlier assisted.

We often find that the more limited the data, the more artful a gifted thinker will become. As though to assert his sovereignty he chooses a few agreeable favorites from the limited number of facts and skillfully marshals the rest so they never contradict him directly. Finally he is able to confuse, entangle, or push aside the opposing facts and reduce the whole to something more like the court of a despot than a freely constituted republic. (Goethe, 1988: pp. 11–17)

It is well to keep in mind that every experiment allows many interpretations, depending upon the points of view we bring to it. For example, when Avery and his co-workers published their article on DNA, the results were by no means universally interpreted as showing that DNA is the substance of genes (see Olby, 1994, pp. 169–206). Those who held protein to be the prime candidate for this substance were not easily convinced. And more generally, couldn't DNA be in some way *changing* (mutating) genes and thereby only indirectly affecting heredity? In retrospect—taking into account reigning theories and all the research that has been done subsequently—*we* see the results as a clear indication that DNA is the substance of the genes. (My students rarely give the "correct" interpretation of this experiment, and I then realize how I expect a narrow, clear-cut interpretation, because I already "know" the answer.)

But an experiment is not understood only in terms of our point of view; it can also stimulate us to ask new questions and frame new ideas. Those scientists who *were* convinced by the experiments of Avery and others now looked at DNA in a new light. They had a new idea—DNA is the substance of genes—and this idea bred new conceptual and experimental activity.

A *way of viewing things* is an intrinsic—even if widely ignored—part of every body of scientific knowledge. Object-thinking is particularly inclined to forget this, instead treating its experimental results as "the objective facts." The way of viewing and the experimental process are seen merely as means to an end. The posited "objective facts" are meant to transcend the personal, shedding the signature of the process out of which they arose.

But this ideal is an illusion. I do not mean that the whole project is arbitrary and "merely subjective." Neither the term "objective" nor "subjective" describes the experimental process. Scientific understanding includes both the receiving of a given that appears independent of the knower, and a creative grasping or apprehending on the part of the knower.

Interestingly, when a scientist calls quantifiable results "objective," it is because mathematics can yield clear agreement among different investigators. Two clear thinkers who follow the same train of mathematical logic will come to the same conclusion. But the reason for this objective certainty lies precisely in the fact that both thinkers can experience the logic of the demonstration from the inside—in thought. So quantifiable phenomena—objective facts—gain their inner sense and their persuasive force from human involvement.

We enter a different relation to our work once we become conscious of our inescapable involvement in the creation of facts. It is no longer possible to retreat behind the authoritative facade of an objective, value-free science.

The facts are connected to us whether we recognize the connection or not. To be responsible is to stand for what we think and do, and for the results of those thoughts and deeds. Although we habitually disregard ethical considerations until a particular result is seen to have negative effects, the ethical dimension in fact remains part of the whole endeavor from its outset, because the scientist remains part of the endeavor (cf. Edelglass et al., 1992). This will become clearer throughout the rest of our discussion.

Taking Organisms in Hand

Every organism has its own characteristics. The experimenter must respond to these characteristics; otherwise, the organism will do badly or die. Understandably, scientists will look for those organisms they can most easily use for their purposes. The history of genetics shows that many genetic discoveries were made because appropriate organisms were used whose characteristics fit the experimental program.

The descriptions that follow are in no way comprehensive. Rather, the few examples are meant to give an impression, first, of the increasing manipulative power that has arisen through the choice of experimental organisms, and, second, of the path that has led from the whole organism to physiology, and finally to substance.

Mendel found the pea to be a good plant to experiment with for a number of reasons. It possessed the distinct traits he was looking for. It allowed cross-pollination in a fashion that, though laborious, left little danger of contamination by unwanted, foreign pollen. The resulting hybrids were always fertile. Pea plants are easy to cultivate, in field experiments as well as in pots.

The pea appears to be an ideal organism for experimentation until one compares it with the workhorse of classical genetics, the fruit fly (*Drosophila melanogaster*). At about one-eighth of an inch long, the fruit fly requires a magnifying glass or low power microscope for trait observation—a disadvantage. But in many respects it is ideal for experimental purposes. Thousands of flies can be held in little "fly rooms" of laboratories around the world; hundreds can be kept in a single jar. Laboratories in Moscow and Buenos Aires can keep *Drosophila* under essentially the same conditions without difficulty. They can be fed an inexpensive, simple nutrient medium containing primarily corn. One female lays hundreds of eggs at a time, and these develop within two to three weeks (depending on the room temperature) into sexually mature flies. One can therefore perform many breeding experiments within a short period of time—experiments that would take years with most plants.

Bacteria

Bacteria, the smallest forms of life, bring yet further advantages to the study of genes. In nature bacteria make themselves known to us almost exclusively through their cumulative effects, particularly through the transformation and decomposition of organic matter. The vinegar-like smell exuding from the apples around which fruit flies hover comes from substances that bacteria produce when breaking down sugar in apples. You might have seen bacteria without knowing it—as a thin film on the surface of a stagnant puddle or pond. If you look at this film under a microscope, you will see countless tiny little dots and lines (the individual bacteria), each about one- to two-thousandths of a millimeter in size. (The smallest object we can see with the naked eye is about one-tenth of a millimeter.) Their minute size again seems less than ideal for experimental purposes. However, one does not experiment with a single bacterium, but rather with populations of millions that are seen as colonies.

Bacterial colonies can be grown under quite simple conditions. Take a petri dish (a transparent, covered dish about the size of a cup saucer) and add a simple nutrient medium containing sugar, minerals, and water. Leave the dish open overnight, and then cover it and put it in an incubator at 37° C (98° F). When you observe the dish the next day, you will find many little circles of various colors and sizes (up to one-quarter inch). These circles are colonies of bacteria, each consisting of millions of individual bacteria (figure 16).

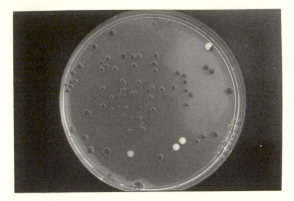

FIGURE 16. Bacterial colonies growing on a nutrient medium in a petri dish. Many dark colonies and four white colonies of the same species (*Rhodopseudomonas capsulata*) are visible. The white colonies are mutants, having lost the capacity to produce a pigment enabling the bacteria to perform photosynthesis (courtesy of L. Margulis).

Where have these colonies come from? Evidently there were bacteria in the air, or already on the petri dish, which found good conditions for growth in the warmed nutrient medium. Bacteria reproduce by division. Under the favorable conditions described above, one bacterium divides into two every thirty minutes, so overnight millions can develop.

Plants reproduce within months at best, fruit flies need only two to three weeks, and bacteria only hours. This acceleration in reproductive rate has led to an acceleration in experimentation. Results come much more quickly.

Depending on conditions in the petri dish, which the scientist can control, different types of bacteria will thrive. For example, bacteria resistant to penicillin are cultivated on media with penicillin; all other bacteria die and only resistant colonies develop. Bacteria thus afford the experimenter a great deal of control, as long as sterile conditions are maintained to prevent contamination by unwanted bacteria omnipresent in our environment.

The genetic traits considered in peas and fruit flies were, until recently, morphological—flower or eye color, seed or wing form, and so on. Bacterial traits are observed indirectly; for example, the ability to grow on a medium with only one specific type of sugar. As we saw in the case of antibiotic resistance, such traits are discovered by changing the medium in which the bacteria grow. The traits do not simply appear; conditions have to be created under which they can be made apparent. In this way the traits of the organism emerge as part of the experimental process. They are not given.

The sequence—peas, fruit flies, bacteria—means accelerated reproduction of ever smaller organisms that take up less space, cost less, and are easier to care for. To interrupt an experiment with bacteria, you can put them in a refrigerator for a few days, taking them out when the experiment is to resume. Manipulating a plant's reproduction requires more knowledge. In this respect, bacteria can be taken more fully in hand than any plants or animals. Moreover, bacteria are, as it were, specialists in physiology, breaking down and building up substances. The physiological functions of bacteria can be utilized in genetic experiments in a way that is not possible with plants and animals. For example, genetic material from other organisms can be introduced into bacterial cells, where it undergoes replication (gene cloning).

Viruses

At the end of the last century scientists discovered agents that were correlated with diseases in plants and animals. When a fluid extract was made from diseased tissue and then injected into another specimen of the same species, this specimen usually became ill. Since such extracts retained their efficacy even when passed through a bacteria-trapping filter, the agent of this efficacy was distinct from bacteria. It was therefore given a name of its own—"virus," the Latin word for poison.

Viruses—such non-bacterial fluid extracts—were defined by other negative characteristics. The extract did not grow in a nutrient medium, and it revealed nothing under the highest magnification of a light microscope. The "disease" of bacteria conditioned by viral agents is confirmed only when one sees holes in bacterial colonies growing in a petri dish.

Viruses were thus known and dealt with, not as entities or organisms, but by their effects on organisms, much as one deals with a chemical substance. But from early on there were scientists who assumed that the basis of the tissue holes lay in tiny, undiscovered entities. After the invention of the electron microscope in the early 1930s, and after researchers succeeded in bringing the tobacco mosaic virus into crystallized form in 1939, it finally became possible to see such an entity. Electron-microscope pictures of viruses are usually magnified fifty thousand to two hundred thousand times.

Virus particles are completely inert outside of living cells. In their failure to grow in a nutrient medium, they are like crystals or chemicals. When, however, they come into contact with living cells, they can, under appropriate conditions, penetrate the cell. Entirely dependent upon the cell's metabolism for substances and energy, the viruses replicate, the cell dies, and new virus particles are freed. Virus replication can be even more rapid than bacterial reproduction: a susceptible bacterium infected by a virus can be dead within twenty minutes, freeing twenty to three hundred new viruses.

Chemical analysis of viruses shows they consist of a protein "body" surrounding a "core" of DNA (or its chemical relative, RNA). In this respect they are like the chromosomes; they have been called wandering genomes, or parasites at a genetic level. They can essentially be seen as, and treated in laboratory experiments like, DNA or another biochemical substance. Therefore, their utility for particular types of genetic experiments and manipulations is hardly surprising. Given their capacity to invade cells, they can deliver foreign genes (genes that may have been cloned by bacteria) into other organisms.

From viruses to the substance of genes is only a small step. The nearer we come to substance, the greater the manipulative power and the fewer the living characteristics of organisms to which the scientist must respond.

DNA: Substance As Process and Entity

Biochemical substances are not "found" in organisms like pieces of gold in a treasure chest. Scientists do not just open organisms up, behold the substances, and take them out. The scientist must typically perform manifold operations to arrive at a suitable product, killing the tissue or organism along the way. If DNA is the desired product, then whole organisms (a culture of millions of bacteria or hundreds of fruit flies), tissues (the liver or thymus of a mouse), or tissue cultures (human white blood cells) are taken. The steps are then essentially the same.

Here, for example, is how DNA can be isolated out of a mouse. The mouse is killed and its thymus is immediately frozen (to prevent decomposition). The frozen tissue in a salt solution is homogenized in a mixer for three minutes. The homogenized pulp is centrifuged at three thousand revolutions per minute for ten minutes. A separation takes place, and the more solid precipitate is saved; the more fluid portion is discarded. Centrifugation is usually repeated one or two times. Then a salt solution and alcohol are added, and a milky white precipitate begins to form in the solution. This is "unrefined" DNA, which can be further purified in additional steps by adding specific enzymes or other substances. When alcohol is added again, white threads form, which can be rolled up on a glass rod. One now has DNA in hand!

DNA can be further analyzed in various ways. One important method is gel electrophoresis (figure 17). Specific enzymes are put into a DNA solution to digest, or break down, the DNA further. The DNA is then brought onto a gel, which is placed in an electric field. After a certain amount of time this gel can be bathed in ethidium bromide, making the DNA visible in ultraviolet light. A number of bands appear, not just one conglomeration. Evidently the previous, long strands of DNA have broken into smaller pieces. Each band represents DNA pieces of the same size. This process, repeated, modified, and refined, has led to the identification of single genes. Such gene sequencing has become highly automated in the past few years, and now forms the basis of the Human Genome Project.

This description of DNA isolation shows that, in order to obtain the final substance, a specific set of actions utilizing physical, chemical, and electrical forces is required. At each step the previous state is altered and a particular result of the analysis is isolated. At the end (which is always a matter of stopping; there is no absolute end of analysis) the obtained result bears no similarity to the origin. Someone unfamiliar with the techniques of biochemistry would hardly imagine that the outcome of such intricate, destructive manipulations could be anything other than a meaningless fragment.

FIGURE 17. Gel electrophoresis. The photograph shows a scientist observing bands of DNA in ultraviolet light. See text for further explanation (from MPG–Spiegel, 3/91).

DNA as an isolated laboratory substance is inert and, if protected from contamination, can be stored (frozen or refrigerated) indefinitely. Whether it came from a bacterium, a plant, or a human being can be seen only on the bottle's label. This DNA has been produced by means of an analytical *process*; as an *entity* in the laboratory, it tells us nothing about its nature.

How, then, are we to learn about DNA's significance in an organism, if it is necessary to analyze the organism—that is, disintegrate the context—in order to obtain the substance? We can only bring it back into another organism and see what "it" does. But this "it" is no longer an isolated substance, and it has been placed in a new context. We can speak of it being in the organism only inasmuch as we discover processes in the organism that have changed.

Substances in organisms are processes, not entities. If we want to show that a substance, conceived as an entity, is implicated in a set of observed changes, then we must undertake the isolation process once again. But the character and continuity of the substance throughout the stages of this process are accessible only to a thinking that lives between the stages and connects them. The character is not "in" the entity, which, as collected material, reveals only one aspect of the substance.

The involvement already considered in connection with the experimental method reaches a climax in the case of substances. Only through activity of the experimenter do biochemical substances arise. As isolated entities, as separate phenomena, these substances are uninteresting. Our knowledge comes by watching interactions and then noting effects. The analytical process that leads to the isolated entity belongs just as much to the concept of the given substance as do the effects (symptoms such as growth or behavioral changes) that arise in an organism when the entity has disappeared into it.

This description may seem unusual, because our familiar object-thinking projects all attributes of substance onto the entity, from which all effects are assumed to radiate. Such a habit of thought does not do justice to the observed phenomena. The realm of biochemical substance is preeminently one of fluidity, not only in the literal sense (which is certainly the case), but more generally in the sense of process, or transformation. While scientists deal practically with this fluidity in experimentation, and abstract from it in describing the effects of a substance in an organism, when object-thinking they ignore it in their fundamental scientific concepts because those concepts concede reality only to mechanically interacting entities.

Creating Conditions

Avery and his co-workers (see chapter 3) succeeded in transforming one strain of bacteria into another by means of DNA only because of their ability to create very specific conditions, which they discuss over a couple of pages in their report. For example, the whole process took place in a medium. It was necessary to have serum in the medium; serum from human lungs proved to be most effective. The nutrient part of the medium was broth made from cattle hearts. The bacterial culture itself had to be young, that is, it had to be made up of cells that were quickly dividing.

All of these somewhat mysterious-sounding conditions were essential to the success of the experiment; without them the experiment did not show DNA's transformative power. It was not clear exactly *why* such conditions, established by trial and error, were absolutely necessary. The researchers had some ideas, some of which later proved incorrect. But that is not important. What is important is that the experiment succeeded.

So if one asks "why" a particular substance in a particular amount is taken for a particular experiment, the answer is generally that someone discovered, perhaps by chance, that the experiment works best under such conditions. Others then follow the "recipe." This trial and error is an essential aspect of science dealing with substances.

Even such techniques as gel electrophoresis or x-ray crystallography can be considered "crafts" or "exacting trades"

(Maddox, 1990; and Braenden and Jones, 1990). They involve great skill in the handling of substances and instruments. One must create optimal conditions to obtain results.

Of course, the more automated our techniques become, the more our previous direct involvement is transferred to machines. In the machine a product of our intelligence takes on a semi-independent existence. Nonetheless, experimental science always bears the signature of human involvement. Only in the popular imagination does the purely objective, uninvolved scientist exist—the beholder of "the way things are."

CHAPTER FIVE

Genetic Manipulation in the Context of Life

Once we have conceived the gene as an independent unit of heredity, it is logical to think about exchanging genes between organisms. If the mechanisms are the same in all organisms, why shouldn't we exchange parts? This hope represents the natural goal of object-thinking—a goal now being attained through genetic engineering.

> The End of our Foundation is the knowledge of Causes and secret motions of things, and the enlarging of the bounds of Human Empire, to the effecting of all things possible.... And we make (by art) in the same orchards and gardens trees and flowers to come earlier or later than their seasons, and to come up and bear more speedily than by their natural course they do. We make them also by art greater much than their nature, and their fruit greater and sweeter and of differing taste, smell, color, and figure, from their nature. And many of them we so order as they become of medicinal use.... We have also parks and enclosures of all sorts of

beasts and birds. . . . By art likewise we make them
greater or taller than their kind is, and contrariwise
dwarf them, and stay their growth; we make them
more fruitful and bearing than their kind is, and contrariwise barren and not generative. Also we make
them differ in color, shape, activity, many ways. . . .

This description was written by the spiritual father of the
experimental method, Francis Bacon, in 1624 (Bacon,
1980). It affords a glimpse of Bacon's New Atlantis, an
imaginary culture of the future based on scientific ideals.
Although traditional breeding techniques have long been
capable of producing new plant and animal varieties, it is
only since the advent of genetic engineering in 1973 that
we are gaining the manipulative power that Bacon
dreamed of.

In the past twenty years it has become possible to transfer genes from organisms of any kingdom into organisms
of any other kingdom. New, "transgenic" (genetically engineered) organisms are being produced daily in laboratories around the globe. Bacteria "manufacture" human
insulin. Parts of transgenic tobacco plants glow in the dark
under laboratory conditions—a dubious distinction
endowed upon them by genes from fireflies. Mice injected
with rat DNA grow larger. Various transgenic plants show
resistance to particular herbicides and microorganisms.
Genetically altered tomatoes can ripen longer on the plant
without getting soft. Work is in progress to create blue
roses. In one experiment, transgenic fruit flies lived longer
than their normal cousins. Fruit flies with legs where their
antennae should be or with eyes on their wings and legs
have been produced in the lab. All this has been achieved
in a relatively brief period.

Technically, the work has proceeded at the level of substance—the level of genes. It is important to gain a concrete picture of this work, and of the complexity of its results. It is all too easy to visualize genetic engineering as a simple, mechanical procedure for removing and replacing genes that have cut-and-dried causal effects. Such pictures, propagated by scientists and journalists alike, answer to object-thinking—but not, as we may have come to expect, to the phenomena themselves.

The Opaque Background of Manipulation

Animal cells have sex chromosomes, which means that the gender of an animal is in most cases correlated with certain chromosomes. In mammals, geneticists speak of the XY male sex chromosomes and the XX female sex chromosomes, in which the sex-determining genes are thought to reside. In particular, researchers have identified one region of the Y-chromosome, called the sex-determining region (abbreviated "Sry" in mice).

The question arose, Might it be possible to turn female mice into males by transferring the sex-determining region of the Y-chromosome into fertilized eggs (Koopman, et al., 1991)? In May, 1991, the cover of the scientific journal *Nature* showed a mouse whose testicles were clearly visible. The caption read, "Making a Male Mouse."

How is such a mouse made? Briefly, as follows:

First, the researcher needs a sufficient amount of Sry DNA. DNA from mice is isolated and the Sry region is separated from the rest. This Sry region is then biochemically attached to bacterial DNA (plasmid-DNA), which in turn is put into a culture of growing bacteria. If conditions are suitable, it is then possible to isolate larger amounts of the

Sry DNA. In what is called gene cloning through bacteria, the bacteria's metabolism produces many "copies" of the mouse DNA by treating it as part of their own genome.

Now the second step: injection of the DNA into fertilized mice eggs. This may sound simple, but it is a complicated and delicate procedure. Female mice are given hormones to induce the maturation of many eggs (superovulation). They are then mated. One day later fertilized eggs are removed from the oviducts. These eggs are only 0.1 millimeter in diameter—the size of a needle tip. The compact head of the sperm has swollen and forms the male nucleus within the cytoplasm of the egg. Under a microscope the Sry DNA is injected into the male nucleus that is ready to fuse with the egg's nucleus. When the nuclei fuse, fertilization is complete and the new organism begins its embryonic development.

The fertilized eggs remain in cultures in the lab overnight. The next day the researcher selects those that have developed to the two-cell stage. These embryos are implanted into   oviducts of "pseudopregnant recipients." Then follows the three-week gestation period.

In the experiment reported in *Nature*, ninety-three mice were born. DNA from their tissues was analyzed to determine whether they had taken up the foreign DNA and become transgenic. Five of the ninety-three mice were transgenic. Two of these were normal XY-males; they were not more masculine because of the extra Sry DNA. Another two of the transgenic mice were normal XX-females; while "both carried many copies of Sry," there was no sex reversal. In these four cases one would have expected changes, but there were none.

One transgenic mouse—the mouse on the journal's cover—was female (XX) with regard to the chromosomes in her body's cells, but male in anatomy and behavior. Only here did sex reversal occur, presumably influenced by the Sry DNA. This mouse's testicles were very small and he was sterile. His mating behavior was, however, completely normal male behavior.

It is truly astounding that scientists can bring about such a significant change as sex reversal. But if we do not fix our attention merely on the one successful result (successful, that is, from the researchers' standpoint), many riddles stare back at us. One concerns the fact that four of the five transgenic mice showed no changes at all. The two transgenic female mice "should" have been male. A more feministically oriented publication could well have put this interesting result in the foreground with the caption, "female mice resist attempt at male domination." One's universe of concern can determine how one looks at a result. In any case, when we survey all the varying results of this experiment, it is obvious that we cannot claim to understand them. No simplistic, "genes determine traits" model is adequate.

Incorporated DNA often disturbs normal processes. For example, in another experiment DNA related to the synthesis of sheep-wool protein was injected into fertilized mouse eggs. The one mouse out of which the most sheep DNA could be isolated was anything but woolly; it suffered cyclical hair loss, and its hair broke prematurely (Powell and Rogers, 1990). This shows in a dramatic way what applies to all genetic engineering experiments: their results cannot be predicted.

A few years ago the first gene-transfer experiment with cattle was performed applying the methods used to produce transgenic mice (Krimpenfort et al., 1991). The researchers used human-derived DNA associated with the formation of an iron-binding protein called lactoferrin. The main purpose of the experiment was to see whether the methods used with mice would work with cattle. In the long run, the aim is to have stocks of transgenic cattle producing pharmaceutical proteins that can be isolated from their milk.

The researchers gave exact numbers at each step of their procedure. This is rarely done—I assume this is because such numbers do not seem essential. In the case of the cattle:

2,470   cow eggs were used, of which
2,297   matured.
1,358   eggs were fertilized (in vitro).
1,154   eggs were injected with human DNA.
  981   survived this procedure.
  687   embryos began embryonic development (cleavage).
  129   embryos were transferred into oviducts of cows.
   21   cows became pregnant.
   19   calves were born.
    2   calves were transgenic.

One of the transgenic calves was actually only partially transgenic. The researchers isolated and analyzed DNA from the placenta, blood, and ear tissue, but the foreign DNA could be detected only from the placenta. Moreover, "a rearrangement had occurred involving a deletion of part of the [foreign] DNA construct."

These results from all of the experiments discussed show that we do not control what occurs in the organism. The surgical and analytical procedures are precise and well defined, but once the threshold between laboratory procedure and organism is breached, everything becomes opaque. The life of the organism takes over, exhibiting a certain autonomy despite all manipulation. Even if the effects of our actions penetrate into the organism, our understanding does not.

The processes may be wasteful—in general, they show about a 1% success rate—but what is important to the genetic engineer is that at least one fertile transgenic organism is produced. The characteristics of this organism can then be multiplied through breeding, so that a stock of transgenic organisms is built up. This sustainable alteration against a background of mystery constitutes the genetic engineer's success.

The Organism in Its Environment

Once transgenic organisms leave the regulated confines of the laboratory, we have a problem similar to that of genes leaving the test tube and entering the organism. We don't know what the interaction with the environment will bring.

In the spring of 1990 the first large-scale experiment in growing transgenic plants outdoors was begun in Germany (MacKenzie, 1990). Maize-derived DNA associated with red pigment formation had been implanted into petunias. When this manipulation was successful, the petunia flowers turned salmon red. The researchers predicted that very rarely a jumping gene would insert itself into the maize gene, blocking its function. As a result, the flowers of such plants would become wholly or partially white instead of red.

Experiments in greenhouses brought the predicted results, but there were too few white flowers to permit further study. A large-scale experiment was needed. In May thirty thousand transgenic petunias were planted in an outside plot. The plants grew and came to flower. Most flowers were red. Some were mottled (variegated) with red and white patches, and some were completely white. But, there were many more white flowers than predicted— about ten times too many.

Then came the next surprise. During a heat wave in July and August the flowers of *all* the plants turned white. Such color bleaching in petunias is not unexpected under such conditions. Normally, the flower pigmentation would later return, but here it happened only with some of the plants; eight times more plants remained with white and mottled flowers than there had been before the period of color bleaching.

To add to the surprise, genetic investigation of seventeen white-flowered plants in the fall showed no indication of a jumping gene. Evidently the whiteness was environmentally induced.

Nothing ran according to plan. Of course, this is not unusual in experimental science, and the researchers now had a whole new set of questions. But this experiment does vividly illustrate that, as long as we manipulate organisms possessing a life of their own in active interplay with the environment, our ability to predict their development will be as limited as the narrow genetic models upon which we base the predictions.

Concerns about the release of transgenic organisms revolve mainly around the possible exchange of genetic material between transgenic and wild organisms. Will transgenic pesticide-resistant plants exchange genetic material with their wild cousins, making the latter resistant as well? Will viruses used as vectors to bring foreign genetic material into an organism recombine with wild viruses and consequently become harmful to the host organism?

Some field trials with transgenic plants suggest that such exchange occurs, while other studies find no evidence for it (Stone, 1994). In a laboratory experiment, transgenic plants carrying a segment of a viral gene were inoculated with a virus strain that was missing precisely this segment (Greene and Allison, 1994). Without the segment, the virus could not infect the whole plant. After inoculation a few plants were completely infected by the virus, which suggests that the virus had combined with the gene segment from the transgenic plant.

Once one begins dealing with viruses and bacteria, the risk is compounded by their minute size and the possibility of rapid, wide distribution. When a strain of bacteria in the United States first becomes resistant to a new antibiotic, it takes only a few weeks for the same resistance to be found in Europe (Wirz, 1992, p. 11).

When genetically engineered bacteria were first produced in laboratories in the 1970s, there was concern that these bacteria might be unwittingly released into the environment. Procedures were established to isolate laboratory strains. In addition, some researchers argued that laboratory bacteria adapted to lab conditions would not be likely to survive outside the lab. But we now know that this is not necessarily the case (Dykhuizen, 1990; Dixon, 1992). For example, a strain of the intestinal bacterium *Escherichia coli* was grown at 42°C—5 °warmer than our normal body temperature. The strain adapted to this higher temperature after sixty days. Surprisingly, when the same strain was subsequently returned to a 37° environment, it grew better than the controls. That is, after adapting to higher temperatures, it also grew better at the lower temperatures (Bennett et al., 1990). A completely unexpected result that counsels restraint.

Since livestock remain more isolated than plants and microorganisms, there is less concern about their potential effects on the environment. But other concerns remain:

> Pigs that were implanted with the gene for human growth hormone showed joint and muscle damage due to their increased size and weight. Normal behavior was almost impossible. When the objection was raised that such a manipulation was not only injurying the pigs' health and causing them pain, but was also compromising their inherent dignity, the answer was given that they could be penned in such a way that they would no longer need to carry out most of their behaviors. (Wirz, 1992, p. 13; my translation)

All these examples show that genetic manipulation of organisms does not succeed in cleanly engineering isolated traits. Rather, the whole organism and its relation to its environment is at stake.

The Importance of Language

Before reading the descriptions in the preceding sections, you might have imagined genetic engineering to be an exact, well-understood, mechanical procedure. It is often presented this way. We hear of genes being *cut* or *spliced* by enzymes, and of new DNA combinations being *manufactured* and *inserted* into the cell. The cell incorporates the DNA into its *machinery*, which begins to *read information* that is *encoded* in the new DNA. This *information* is then *expressed* in the *manufacture* of corresponding proteins that have a particular function in the organism. And so, as if resulting from such precisely determinate procedures, the transgenic organism takes on new traits.

Such language is on the one hand mechanomorphic (*cutting, machinery, manufacture*) and on the other hand anthropomorphic (*information, code, expression*). The combination of the two makes it sound as though one could actually see and understand all that is going on. In reality this language is a crutch and puts a veil over the actual phenomena. If you visit a genetic engineering laboratory, you may be disappointed to find that none of the processes described above can be observed. This is not because the *cutting* is being hidden, but because it is occurring in thought. There is, in fact, little to see in a gene lab.

Concerning the relationship between phenomenon and interpretation, the following example is instructive. In the original article about the first successful case of genetic engineering, Cohen et al. write about enzymes cleaving DNA into fragments. Specific enzymes and DNA—both in fluid state—are combined. The DNA is then subjected to gel electrophoresis as described previously. One then sees the small bands representing the DNA. In one case Cohen et al. write, "Only one band is observed . . . suggesting that this plasmid [DNA ring from bacteria, CH] has only a single site susceptible to cleavage" (Cohen et al., 1973). Two years later, in a more popular article in *Scientific American*, Cohen writes about the same experiment: "We found that the enzyme had cut the plasmid in only one place, producing a linear fragment" (Cohen, 1975). The more tentative and careful formulation of the original publication lets the reader distinguish between observation and interpretation. The popular version two years later describes the experiment as if the researchers had directly observed a fact of sense experience (the DNA is *cut*, producing a *linear fragment*).

Genes and Metaphors

Discussing the role of genes in development, Nijhout writes,

> In genetics and developmental biology, powerful and evocative metaphors about genetic controls and genetic programs describe our intuition about the relations between genes and the processes that lead to biological form. The evocative power of these metaphors, however, tends to make us forget that they are no more than working hypotheses. In particular, now that their use has become widespread among biologists, it has become ever easier to believe that the jargon represents understanding and that the metaphors describe the mechanism rather than the model.
>
> (Nijhout, 1990)

"My soul is an enchanted boat" (Shelley). This is a metaphor. No one will accuse Shelley of literally equating the soul with a boat. The enchanted boat is in itself a powerful image. When we connect it to the concept of the soul as Shelley does, then, in the tension of this connection, we can fathom a new dimension of the meaning of soul. The metaphor points to something beyond the literal meanings of its terms.[1]

I don't think that most scientists take their statements about genes to be metaphorical; they are meant literally—that is, they are taken as descriptions of external facts. This is where the problem arises. "From DNA issue the commands that regulate the nature and number of virtually

---

1. For in-depth consideration of the nature of metaphors, see Barfield, 1973; Wheelwright, 1962; Wheelwright, 1968.

every type of cellular molecule" (Watson et al., 1983, p. 1). This is meant to be a statement of fact. But we do not observe DNA giving commands. We *interpret* the facts as commands.

When we speak of commands, our thinking is governed, consciously or otherwise, by the image of a knowing agent who has some purpose in mind, who effectively communicates his intentions to others, and who marshals his resources with his purposes in mind. Of course, none of this is permissible within a scientific model, so it must be concealed in generally accepted metaphors. Such metaphors help us preserve the appearance of mechanism (insofar as we mistake the metaphors for literalisms), while at the same time they grant us the satisfaction of a model that is meaningful and effective—if also illicit (because the metaphors draw their force from meanings that mere objects cannot support).

The greatest injustice is done to the public through misleading popularization. When, for example, diagrams of genetic models are presented, it is usually impossible for lay readers to know that they are looking, not at a phenomenon, but rather at the writer's interpretation. Simplified presentations that materialize mental constructs are often seen as a pedagogical tool to make things more understandable. It may be true that readers gain greater clarity, but what they understand so clearly is only the model given by object-thinking.

There is a real danger that we are unwittingly teaching students and the public to be naive believers in the "hard facts" of science (which, unknown to them, are usually model-permeated), instead of stimulating them to be critical thinkers who embody the true spirit of scientific inquiry. Presentations of genetics—and scientific matters in general—become truly pedagogical when they break the confines of object-thinking and illuminate genetics as a living process. This means including the questions, procedures, mistakes, hopes, and unfiltered results, as well as the scientist's models.[2]

I have described the language of genetics as mechanomorphic and anthropomorphic. The former imbues descriptions with solidity and clarity, the latter with meaning. With this language, geneticists try to reconstruct the reality they previously sacrificed in the process of analysis. Analysis alone destroys meaningful connections. In genetic engineering experiments, a new context for the isolated products of analysis arises through the living host organism. But this living background remains largely inaccessible to the researchers, who substitute for it by framing their concepts mechanically and anthropomorphically.

DNA in the Life of the Organism

In space, two objects exist side by side, enclosed within their own boundaries. If they interact as objects, then these interactions are external and can be described in mechanical terms, as when one object hits the other, setting it in motion. If water is carelessly poured onto a plant, then the plant's stem may break. I can describe this process in terms of mass, velocity, direction, elasticity, and so on. That the plant is a living organism does not figure

---

2. In my experience, students can clearly grasp and apply the distinction between phenomena and models only when they are about sixteen or seventeen years old—in the eleventh grade. When models are taught before this age, they tend to be taken as facts, so that we are sowing the seeds of misplaced concreteness, ending up with students who believe, for example, that atoms and molecules are made up of little balls.

in these considerations because I am looking only at its object nature.

If, however, water penetrates the soil and the plant's living roots take it up, the object relationship is overcome. When the plant incorporates water into its growth processes, the water ceases to be an object. We are all familiar with the appearance of a plant that lacks water—wilted, yellowing leaves and limply hanging stems; growth has stopped. When the rains come, the plant swells with water, the leaves spread, the stems straighten. The plant begins to grow again. Water that was outside the plant has now become part of it.

Every organism is continuously going beyond a mere object relation to its surroundings. What was outside is now inside—not inside as in a drawer filled with things, but, rather, inside as incorporation, as unification.

The plasticity whereby an organism selectively incorporates aspects of its environment, internalizing them and entering into a nonobject-like relation with them, is an essential characteristic of life. This plasticity is a prerequisite for all genetic research and genetic manipulation. Without an egg's ability to take DNA into itself, no genetic manipulation could succeed. This capacity is *utilized* in genetic engineering, but not adequately *recognized* due to the focus on DNA and on the selected results of manipulation.

If conditions are appropriate in a forest, a seed will germinate and a plant will begin to develop. The forest ecosystem provides forces and substances out of which the plant creates its body. In this sense the forest brings forth the plant. The forest's general potential to nurture plants is rendered specific by the particular seed.

European settlers arriving in North America unintentionally brought myriad seeds of wildflowers with them.

The seeds of "weeds" were mixed with the grain they brought to sow in their new homeland. Some of these new plants thrived. Today many wildflowers we find in New England fields and especially along roadsides are "alien"— that is, of European origin: Queen Anne's lace, wild chicory, and the all-pervasive dandelion. Some alien species have become established in forests. Through these new species the forest takes on a different character, while at the same time providing the conditions without which the plant could not live.

The relation between seed and forest is similar to the mutual dependency between DNA and its host organism. DNA requires the nurturing environment of the organism while itself channeling the organism's capacities in a specific direction.

You will remember the two aspects of heredity we discussed in chapter 1: the organism's overall, plastic potential for development on the one hand, and on the other hand its specificity, which limits potential. Clearly, DNA serves as an integral part of the processes specifying particular characteristics. DNA is associated with a particular eye color, a particular hormone, a particular protein. When DNA associated with the formation of a protein that helps dissolve blood clots in human beings is incorporated by goats and the goats secrete this protein in their milk, then the goat has a new characteristic. The goat's metabolism is focused and specified in a new way by the incorporation of DNA; analogously, the forest community takes on a new coloring when a new species is introduced into it.

Looked at in this way, DNA is a significant substance associated with the fixity of characteristics in an organism. Therefore it complements an organism's fluid plasticity.

But this does not mean that we can explain species through genes. A species—a dandelion, a pea, or a fruit fly—is characterized by a particular configuration of characteristics. When we have assembled a list of traits—red eyes, six legs, body bristles, and so on—we do not have the species, because the list does not tell us how the parts are configured to form a whole. The methods of genetics entail abstracting from the species in order to determine and follow the hereditary patterns of isolated traits.

Any given characteristic or segment of DNA might be isolated from another organism. And because the isolated DNA does not carry the stamp of the species, DNA can cross species and kingdom boundaries without being rejected by the host organism's immune system. DNA is interchangeable, but species are not; they are individual. Contemporary genetic research does not lead to an understanding of species.

It is important to recognize this boundary of genetic understanding, since, by altering species through genetic engineering, we may someday produce transgenic organisms that are deemed new species. We may look to such prospects with fear or excitement, but, in any case, if we rely on genetic thinking alone, we will certainly not understand what we have ushered into being.

Transgenic Organisms Reflect the Way We Think

The seeds of most plants are dependent on particular conditions. Few species that grow in a moist, bottomland forest can be found in a dry, exposed forest at the top of a neighboring hill. This is where the plant relates to its environment differently from the way introduced DNA relates to its host organism. Organisms must be treated in specific ways and at particular times to facilitate an interaction with foreign DNA. This is rather like preparing the soil and choosing the right time to sow a seed. But, in contrast to most seeds, DNA from any given "setting"—bacteria, corn, or mice—can "thrive" in any other setting. Nevertheless, examples like light-radiating plants seem to me a bit like water lilies growing in the desert—completely out of context.

Clearly, there is no plant-related reason to radiate light, nor is there a fly-related reason to have legs where the antennae should be. The accessory legs are formed at the cost of the antennae—the fly's organs for its sensitive sense of smell. When such flies arise as mutants, which occasionally happens in nature, they are not viable. We consider them pathological and monstrous.

Through such genetic manipulations we disturb the integrity of the organism as a whole. This follows from our willingness to consider organisms as conglomerations of separate traits. Transgenic organisms put our thinking on display. Object-thinking finds an especially stark reflection in the disjointed, erector-set character of such plants and animals.

The most extreme transgenic forms arise in basic scientific and medical research. The experiment with firefly genetic material in tobacco plants was not done on a whim; rather, the firefly DNA had been biochemically attached to other DNA, and the capacity to glow was used as a "reporter" of the latter's expression—that is, to make visible what would otherwise have remained invisible (Ow et al., 1986). Likewise, the mouse with cyclical hair loss was the unexpected result of an experiment to investigate the formation of wool protein (Powell and Rogers, 1990).

Of course, not all transgenic organisms have been so grossly manipulated. But they are still products of object-thinking, which emphasizes a particular trait or function and overlooks the organism as a whole. The organism is reduced to a medium that scientists manipulate to answer their questions.

But genetic engineering presses beyond basic research. If this were not the case, it would remain a fairly remote endeavor. The additional driving forces range from the sincere wish to diagnose, prevent, and heal diseases, to the desire for recognition and perhaps a Nobel prize. And as more products of genetic engineering become marketable, the motive to earn billions of dollars looms larger.

It has become impossible to ignore the moral, social, economic, and ecological implications of the manipulation of life. The web of relationships grows ever more complex, and our choice of viewpoint plays an increasingly critical role.

Just how critical will become more evident as we consider the cow.

The Cow as Organism and Bioreactor

When we drink milk or eat yogurt and cheese, we are consuming products through which we are connected to the work of countless people—the farmers and those who produce the actual products; those who market, sell and distribute them; those who devise and build machines for these activities; and so on.

All this activity radiates out from the cow—the primary source of our milk products. The cow in turn depends upon the meadow grasses and wildflowers to produce its milk. At the same time, the cow's dung fertilizes the plants from which it lives.

Viewing the animal as an organism, Goethe wrote:

Hence we conceive of the individual animal as a small
world, existing for its own sake, by its own means.
Every creature has its own reason to be. All its parts
have a direct effect on one another, a relationship to
one another, thereby constantly renewing the circle of
life. (Goethe, 1988, p. 121)

In this spirit I will briefly describe the cow, following in
part the masterful description by E.M. Kranich (1994).

Cows are grazers. They live in the midst of the food they
eat. The cow lowers its head to the ground and touches the
meadow plants (or the hay in its stall) with the front end of
its soft, moist snout. The cow does not bite off the plants
with its teeth or lips, but reaches out with its rough, muscular tongue, enwraps the plants, and tears them off. It
clearly needs to use its tongue in this way—cattle that
receive soft feed begin to lick their fellow cows much more
than usual. The tongue needs the stimulation of roughage.

After it has torn off a few portions and chewed a bit, the
cow swallows a mouthful. This activity continues for a few
hours. The food reaches the rumen, the huge first chamber of the four-chambered stomach. Occupying the entire
left side of the abdominal cavity, the rumen can hold forty-
five gallons.

Digestion in the rumen is facilitated by microorganisms
that break down cellulose, the main, hard-to-digest component of roughage. Bacterial activity, the secretion of digestive juices, and the muscle activity of the rumen are all
stimulated by roughage. In fact, the rumen only finishes its
development and becomes functional when a calf begins
to feed on grass or hay.

When the rumen is about half-full, portions of the partially digested food are regurgitated back into the mouth. Rumination begins. Cows usually lie on the ground while ruminating. They grind their food between their large cheek teeth in rhythmical, circling motions of the lower jaw. You are probably familiar with the picture of calm presented by a herd of cows, lying in a meadow, their activity focused inwardly on grinding and digestion.

Digestion involves an intensive production, circulation, and secretion of body fluids. The process begins in the head. While the cow is ruminating, the saliva glands secrete copious amounts of saliva—up to forty gallons a day. The drier the feed (for example, hay), the more the saliva, and the greater the amount of water a cow drinks. As Kranich points out, functionally one can consider the mouth to be a fifth chamber of the stomach.

After rumination, the food is swallowed, entering first the other three chambers of the stomach and then the small intestine. In these organs, fluids are removed from the food and new digestive juices are secreted until finally the cow has broken down its food to a point where it can be taken up by the blood.

Characteristic for cows is their fluid dung, in contrast to the solid dung of other ruminants like sheep or deer. The cow's large intestine does not absorb as much fluid out of this final section of the digestive tract. In fact, from its moist snout, through the whole digestive tract, and finally in its dung, the cow shows more fluidity than other ruminants.

The digestive process is related to the blood—a fluid organ that connects all organs of the body. For every quart of saliva, three hundred quarts of blood pass through the salivary glands. The other digestive organs are sustained by a similarly strong circulation.

The intensive transformation of substances and secretion of fluids characterizing the digestive process are heightened in the formation and secretion of milk. Substances produced by digestion are withdrawn from the blood in the udder. For every quart of milk, three to five hundred quarts of blood pass through the udder. Glands in the udder then create a wholly new substance—milk. This is not a substance that is used by the cow or excreted; rather, it serves another growing organism—the calf. The cow only begins to produce milk after she has given birth to a calf, and the calf has begun to suck on the teats.

When we build up a picture of the cow in this way, we begin to see the cow as a total organism. We view each part in the context of other parts, so that the animal as a whole comes into view, even if only in an elementary way. One result of this endeavor is that milk loses its isolated status as a product we consume. As consumers we tend to take for granted our relation to the cow. When we gain some insight into the cow viewed as an organism, this relation is enhanced.

The domestication of cows by human beings goes back thousands of years. In the course of time this interaction has led to many different breeds, each with its own characteristics. These characteristics reflect in part the aims of the breeders. Breeders try to realize in the domestic animal (or plant) a mental picture they carry within themselves. Moreover, the way we now care for these animals stems in good part from our points of view.

Until this century the cow gave about as much milk per day as her calf would have drunk, had it not been weaned—about two to three gallons in present-day breeds (in India, about one-half gallon per day). In our time, the dairy cow's milk production can exceed seven gallons per day. This increase has taken place essentially within the last fifty years.

How has the increase been made possible? First, by breeding larger cows that by virtue of their size eat more, digest more, and give more milk. Second, by feeding them differently. When cows receive more high-protein grains in their feed, they produce more milk. But since, as we have seen, cows need roughage, this dietary change has its limits.

A simple method has been developed to circumvent the need for roughage in steers bred for beef (Loerch, 1991). The steers are "fed" plastic pot scrubbers—the ones we buy in supermarkets—instead of roughage. In trials, pot scrubbers were wrapped in masking tape and then, one after another, eight scrubbers were pushed down the steer's throat into the rumen. The tape soon detached from the scrubbers, which "were observed to float on the surface of the ruminal contents in these steers and to form a mat similar to that observed when ruminants are fed roughage." The scrubbers remain in the rumen for life.

The trials indicated that steers fed 100% concentrate plus pot scrubbers grew at approximately the rate of cattle fed 85% concentrate with 15% roughage (corn silage). Evidently, the scrubbers stimulate the rumen walls in a manner similar to roughage.

In undertaking his research, Loerch surmised that "because roughage is relatively low in energy and is expensive, it would be beneficial if roughage could be eliminated from cattle diets without sacrificing performance." It is by no means clear that a farmer would actually save money using this method, since it is not a given that 15% more concentrate would be cheaper than producing or buying a corresponding amount of corn silage. But some farmers or feedlots have evidently used Loerch's method, since, as a university animal scientist, he is reported to have received many phone calls "from bewildered butchers who have found pot scrubbers in the guts of slaughtered cattle" (*New York Times*, August 29, 1992).

In its starkness this example is illustrative. It shows not only how strongly the desire to lower costs is a determining factor in agricultural research, but also in what narrow terms the cow is viewed. The cow's need for roughage is reduced to a mechanical function, and this can be substituted for. The sensory qualities of hay or silage—taste, smell, texture—are not considered. Nutritional considerations are reduced to ascertaining that roughage is low-calorie feed and therefore not effective for fast growth. The steer can no longer ruminate because the scrubbers are too large to be regurgitated. Has this no significance for the animal's well-being and physiology? The cow as a mechanism and not the cow as an organism stands behind this roughage substitute.

Perhaps a more enlightened age will discover that the nutritional quality of foodstuffs such as milk or beef are dependent not only on the results of biochemical analysis, but also on the way the animals are raised and cared for.

Coupling the view of the cow as a mechanism with a one-sided economic perspective that emphasizes cost-effectiveness has become increasingly prevalent in our times. This is particularly true in genetic engineering:

Producing human pharmaceutical proteins in the milk of transgenic livestock has been an attractive possibility…. Such "molecular pharming" [*ph*-armacy + f-*arming*] technologies are appealing for a number of reasons. They offer the potential of extremely high volumetric productivity, low operating costs, and unlimited multiplication of the bioreactor [that is, the animal].... In this issue of *Bio/Technology* three groups report significant progress in realizing these benefits.... Their results provide convincing demonstration of the feasibility of using animals as commercial bioreactors. (Bialy, 1991)

The attempt to continually increase milk production reflects the treatment of cows as commercial bioreactors. This tuning of the bioreactor in a specific direction has brought with it some unwanted side effects. These include fertility problems, mastitis, and leg and hoof afflictions. High milk-producing cows are often slaughtered after three years of lactation (five-year-old animals). Without the demand to produce as much milk as possible in a short period of time, a cow will reach its peak of milk production after three or four years of lactation, and will continue healthy lactation for a number of years beyond that.

When we begin to think in terms of the organism, we learn to expect that the desired effect of our manipulations will in all likelihood be only one among many changes. From the point of view of the organism, there is no such thing as a side effect. The organism is a whole. If we change a part, the whole is changed, and this change will likely manifest in ways that go beyond any desired effects.

It is not, therefore, very surprising that mastitis can accompany increased milk production. Mastitis is an inflammation of the udder. Since it is an infectious disease, strict hygienic procedures are called for to prevent bacteria from entering the udder via the openings in the teats. But this is only one side of the problem. Due to the intensive circulation in the udder during lactation, the udder is susceptible to inflammation. (Increased circulation always occurs in inflamed organs—it calls forth the warmth and redness of inflamed tissue.) When milk production is increased to the utmost degree, the udder is almost on the verge of inflammation without bacteria. The cow's physiology is stressed, and when bacteria do enter the udder, mastitis is likely.

In November, 1993, the Food and Drug Administration (FDA) approved the commercial sale of milk, milk products, and meat from cows treated with recombinant bovine growth hormone (rBGH). This hormone is produced by bacteria that have been genetically altered by a cow-derived DNA that is related to the organism's production of growth hormone. In some unknown way, growth hormone stimulates milk production. Cows injected with this hormone produce 10 to 20% more milk.

Much controversy surrounds the use of rBGH, and in Europe its use has not been approved. The FDA was concerned solely with the product's safety. FDA scientists concluded that experimental evidence (provided by manufacturers of rBGH) demonstrates that milk from treated cows is in essence chemically identical to milk from untreated cows. Therefore, the FDA sees no reason for the milk to be labeled as coming from rBGH-treated cows.

Extensive testing of rBGH was done on rats as part of the FDA's procedure for establishing the safety of the substance. Although such experimental results cannot simply be assumed to be valid for cows, they are in and of themselves interesting. Researchers found that the whole organism was affected by rBGH. The treated animals were larger than normal. When the researchers investigated the individual organs, they found that some were proportionately smaller while others were proportionately larger than normal. Such changes depended in part on the animal's sex. "Ratios of organ weight to body weight were increased for spleen and adrenal [gland] and decreased for testes in male rats, and increased for heart and spleen and decreased for brain in the female rats" (Juskevich and Guyer, 1990).

Such detailed analyses have not been performed on cows, but the question of the effects of rBGH has been a source of major controversy and concern. Monsanto, a producer of rBGH, claims there are no significant side effects. Some independent scientists have come to different conclusions. Most recently, a research group led by Erik Millstone analyzed Monsanto data. The group concluded that milk from rBGH-treated cows contained an average of 19% more white blood cells than milk from untreated cows (Millstone et al., 1994). White blood cells enter an organ as part of the inflammatory reaction. An increase in white blood cells is "associated with increased risk of mastitis." The researchers acknowledge that their analysis will remain incomplete until Monsanto releases all pertinent data. They also report that Monsanto blocked their original attempt to publish their analysis of the data.

Out of what context is rBGH produced, and into what context do its effects radiate? Clearly, there is no consumer demand for more milk, nor is there a demand for rBGH milk. "From 1987 to 1989 the [U.S.] government has spent between $600 million and $1.3 billion a year to purchase surplus milk" (*Hastings Center Report*, July/August, 1991, p. 3). Moreover, the Congressional Budget Office estimated that if only one in five farmers were to use rBGH in the first year it is sold, "the government will have to spend $15 million [more] to buy the [additional] surplus milk" (*New Scientist*, November 20, 1993, p. 12).

It is absurd to invent a product to increase milk production while milk itself is already being produced in surplus. Such a total separation of production from actual needs is a consequence of our economic system. In modern Western economic ideology there is an emphasis on growth, higher production, and cost-cutting. The attempt to emphasize such things in agriculture has led to the development of ever larger factory farms. Higher productivity is achieved to the detriment of the connection between farmers and the plants and animals upon which their work is based. And large government subsidies reflect an approach to production that does not take into consideration real consumer needs.

Large chemical companies continually grow. This growth is seen as the means to counter rising costs of production (inflation, higher wages, and so on). When such a company invests millions of dollars to develop a new product like rBGH, it must aggressively market the product. Farmers (particularly those with large farms) who seek further mechanization and ever higher production are most likely to use rBGH. But others follow in fear of not being able to compete.

And what about the cow? As long as we treat it as a commercial bioreactor, there is no reason not to continue trying to increase production. But if we remember that the cow is an organism, then we must ask how far we can healthily push milk production. By gaining insight into the cow as a "small world, existing for its own sake," we can recognize its specific characteristics and needs, and begin to fit our actions into its context.

Practicing this point of view is made extremely difficult by current economic realities. This problem, where it is recognized, has led (to mention one example) to the establishment of Community Supported Agriculture (Groh and McFadden, 1990; Lamb, 1994). Here farmers and consumers enter an economic association that frees the farmer to some degree from the compelling necessity to increase production and lower costs. The consumer community provides the farmer with an income. At the same time, farm production is related more directly to consciously affirmed consumer needs. Within this setting it becomes possible to handle animals like the organisms they are.

Anyone who thinks in terms of commercial bioreactors and acts accordingly will of necessity consider it uneconomic to worry over the fact that animals are living, sentient beings.

Taking Responsibility for Our Point of View

The treatment of the cow as a commercial bioreactor illustrates how our actions carry the stamp of a particular way of thinking. Every point of view leads to specific behavior in the world. And yet, scientific practice as such is usually pictured without reference to ethics.

This is not surprising. In object-thinking, I attend to the object alone, and not to my relation to it as knower and doer. But it is precisely this relation that is at issue ethically, as when I ask, for example, "Is it responsible to release genetically engineered organisms into the environment? Can I take responsibility for the effects of such an act?"

Ethical questions simply do not arise in object-thinking. When scientists express ethical concerns, they have left their object-thinking behind. When, on the other hand, they remain wholly immersed in their science, the ethical questions are left to outsiders. Congressman David Obey, for example, threatened to freeze the 153 million dollar human genome budget if the National Institutes of Health did not work harder to protect against misuse of information. "I am very reluctant to put more money into [human genome research] until I am convinced...that the best minds in science and law are focused on getting up to speed on how to handle this information." The genome project director, Francis Collins, was reported to be alarmed (*Science*, March 31, 1995, p. 1895). A typical wake up call from the outside.

The concept of responsibility is eminently contextual. In every action I connect myself with the world. The world then carries my imprint. In this fundamental way I am responsible for everything I do, whether I am aware of it or not.

Most of us will not feel responsible for a tree that falls over in a windstorm. If, however, we had noticed that the tree trunk was rotting before the storm, we might have a bad conscience afterwards and sense that it was irresponsible not to have cut down the tree, because someone might have been hurt. In the first case we hold the tree's falling to be an "act of nature"—external to us and beyond our influence. In the second case we find ourselves bound to the tree by our choices and their effects.

When we sense responsibility, we feel a connection between our thoughts, feelings, or actions and something in the world. We internalize what we might have left "out there." So long as we can hold things at a distance, no feeling of responsibility arises. By the same token, when we deny responsibility, we maintain or create an inner distance between ourselves and the other.

Our responsibility, then, is governed by those very qualities we have discovered in living organisms. Organisms do not relate to their surrounding environment as if it were an object. They internalize what was outside of them, integrating it into themselves. In so doing they change. Similarly, my feeling of responsibility emerges only where an "other" has to some degree ceased to be a mere object. I dwell within it, or it dwells within me.

In our day, science and technology have radical effects upon the world. Yet the scientific methodology insulates itself from these effects by referring essential questions to philosophers and politicians. A responsible science would require of us increased awareness from the outset. We can only *take* responsibility consciously.

This taking of responsibility begins with the awareness of our point of view. There is no compelling necessity to look at the world in a particular way. We choose, and cannot deny that we are connected to the results of our choice (cf. Edelglass et al., 1992, pp. 125ff.).

Reductionism can be practiced responsibly only when we remain aware that, while it allows an exact focus and may lead to an understanding of particulars, it also destroys context. Recognizing this, we will not reify the abstract products of reduction into independent objects separate from us. Rather, we will know them to stand within a larger context of which we and our point of view are also a part.

As it is, reductionist science does not tend to cultivate such awareness. Symptomatic is a "straw poll" a biology professor made of first-year biology students "to see how many of them had come across the notion that, even in these banausic times, there is such a thing as the philosophy of science, and that reductionism constitutes one approach by which one may seek to understand nature. To this end, I asked them if they had come upon the term 'reductionism.' Not one of them had" (Kell, 1991).

It is essential to lead students into a conscious recognition of the specific approach they are pursuing. How can they take responsibility for their way of thinking, and then for the results of that way of thinking, if they know nothing of their own or other points of view? Through lack of critical reflection, reductionism perpetuates itself and ignores the roots of responsibility within the human being.

While proceeding from object-thinking, genetic engineering affects the organism as a whole. An awareness of this whole would lead to greater thoughtfulness and caution. We would ask larger questions about what we are doing, and place our actions into the context of their outward-rippling effects. We would try to accompany the effects of our actions out into the world. After all, no transgenic organism exists without us; we helped it into existence. Are we prepared to live side-by-side with it?

It is unrealistic to suppose that one day we will be able to predict before the fact all the consequences of any scientific or technological endeavor. Life always brings surprises, and we cannot foresee the future through the lens of previous knowledge. So it is all the more essential to imbue an undertaking with a contextual attitude of mind from the outset. This demands wakefulness and the will to change.

CHAPTER SIX

Heredity and
the Human Being

If we were not born in so helpless and germinal a state, if we did not then go through an extended (actually, lifelong) development of physical and mental capacities, which are subject to myriad internal and external influences, if we did not also mold our own lives by struggling to free ourselves from hereditary and environmental determination—in short, if we were not human—it would be much simpler to speak about heredity in the human being.

As it is, there is no human characteristic of which we can say, "this is purely hereditary," or "this is environmental." The difficulty has been pointed out before (see, for example, Hubbard and Wald, 1993; Lewontin, 1991; and Rose et al., 1984), but the desire to see things simply is very strong, so that the absurd dichotomy "nature *or* nurture" is discussed as if it actually existed somewhere other than in the minds of the scientists and journalists who posit it.

I would like to describe one aspect of human development in order to show the rich context of heredity.

Development of the Lower Limbs

An infant often becomes aware of its feet when it bites into its toes for the first time. These organs remain fairly dormant until the child, usually near its first birthday, pulls itself up and stands, or wobbles, upright. With this act the child begins to take hold of its whole body. If one studies the feet and lower limbs, one sees that they are at first by no means adequate instruments for standing and walking.

Figure 18 shows the footprints of two different children. We will consider the arches. The arch of a foot, as

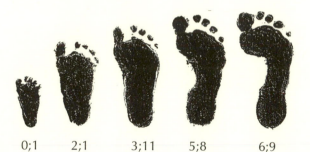

0;1   2;1   3;11   5;8   6;9

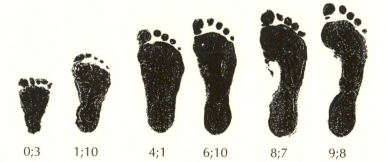

0;3   1;10   4;1   6;10   8;7   9;8

FIGURE 18. Development of the arches in two different children (sibling girls); ages given in years and months.

figures 19 and 20 illustrate, is in reality a complex of three arches: an arch from the inside of the foot to the outside of the foot (transverse arch), a lengthwise arch on the inside of the foot (medial longitudinal arch), and a less pronounced lengthwise arch on the outside of the foot (lateral longitudinal arch). As we see in figure 18, the arches are not very defined until about four years of age or later. In one child the arches are quite pronounced by age seven, and in the other child by eight and one-half years.

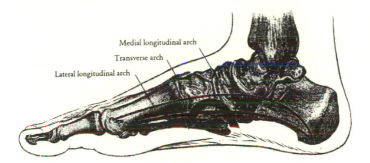

FIGURE 19. The three arches of a foot (from Anthony and Kolthoff, 1975).

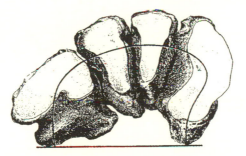

FIGURE 20. The transverse arch as formed by four of the tarsals; left foot, viewed from behind (from Benninghof and Goerttler, 1980).

In the time between the second year of life, when a child begins to stand and walk, and the age of seven or eight, when its arches are essentially developed, the child has also learned to jump, run, and skip. So the feet develop in the context of their usage. We do not first have highly developed feet and legs that are ideal for standing, walking, jumping, running and skipping. Rather, we stand, walk, jump, run, and skip with unfinished instruments that develop in this process. The feet we walk on when we are seven are not ones we inherited.

We all know through our own experience that muscles develop and change according to use. But what we may not realize is that such transformations occur right down into the very bone structure. Figure 21 shows the development of two of the foot bones (the calcaneus or heel bone and the talus, which rests on the calcaneus and connects to the lower leg). The back part of the heel bone is quite round in the newborn; at two years of age it is narrower and more upright; and this process culminates in the narrow, upright orientation of the bone in the adult.

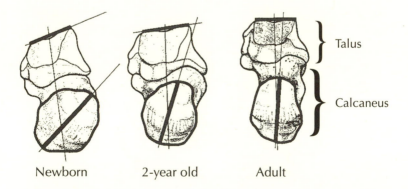

FIGURE 21. Development of two foot bones, showing the marked development in bone structure. The right foot is viewed from behind; the talus rests on the calcaneus (heel bone) (from Benninghof and Goerttler, 1980).

We can also see how the inner (medial) surfaces of the two bones are raised and modeled into part of the arches. Correspondingly, the upper joint surface of the talus becomes horizontal and, functionally speaking, a stable, weight-carrying surface.

It is evident that the foot's development can be understood only in the context of use. This is true of the whole muscular and skeletal system. The term "use" is a very general one, however. We will now look in more detail at some of the influences molding the bones.

First, our bones develop in relation to gravity and to the weight resting upon them. Astronauts suffer a loss of bone density under weightless conditions. X-rays showed, for example, that astronauts who were in space for up to twelve days lost 6% of their heel bone density. "In both Apollo and Skylab programs the decrease in bone density occurred in the calcaneus [heel bone], but not in the radius or ulna [bones of the lower arm], confirming that mineral loss occurs primarily from weight-bearing bones in crew members on all space flights" (Goode and Rambaut, 1985). Our leg and foot bones lose density during prolonged bed rest. Conversely, when we gain weight, the shafts of the long bones of the legs actually increase in diameter.

In addition, the muscles, which are rooted in the bones, continually affect the bones by applying stress during movement. This is reflected in bone structure. Long-time soccer players often have femurs (thighbones) that are larger in diameter than those of nonathletes, and the radius (lower arm bone) of a tennis player's racket arm is larger in diameter than that of the other arm (Larson, 1973).

The effect of disuse is also marked. The shaft of the tibia (shinbone) of a child up to about two years old has a circular form in cross section, whereas that of an adult is triangular. If the muscles of the lower leg are paralyzed at a young age, the circular form persists—"a sign that the functional demands determine the three-edged form" (Benninghof and Goerttler, 1980, vol 1, p. 236; my translation).

That what we inherit as a *hereditary model* (as I will call it, for lack of a better term) is characterized by great plasticity becomes even more evident when we consider hereditarily conditioned disorders that limit this plasticity. Duchenne muscular dystrophy is a degenerative disease of muscular tissue. Affected individuals usually develop normally until they are three years old; then their muscle tissue progressively degenerates, so that they are often wheelchair-dependent by ten or twelve years of age. As a result, the thickness of their bones decreases and the bones suffer osteoporosis, fracturing easily (Hsu, 1982).

This hereditary condition does not allow these individuals to take hold of their bodies in a normal way. Their bodies are like a solid barrier that does not allow penetration. Through this resistance, the relationship to the body becomes more conscious and problematic.

Normal bodily development entails less resistance and less bodily awareness—the adaptation of the body to the function can be taken for granted. Nonetheless, even in healthy development it remains true that when we reach a particular stage of development, that stage is not only a foundation but also a barrier to be overcome in the achievement of new stages.

This fact is wonderfully illustrated by figure 22 which shows the leg bones of an eighteen-month-old boy and the same boy at five years. The transformation is remarkable. At eighteen months, the boy exhibited a so-called physiological bowing of the legs (Holt et al., 1954). Most children who begin to walk have bowed legs, but not in such an extreme fashion. The lower ends of the femurs and the upper ends of the tibias in the illustration show strong flaring on their inner (medial) surfaces. The boy already had bowed legs when he began to walk at eight months. Such bowing increases the compression and stress on the medial surfaces of the bones. The bones answer to this condition, and the medial flaring of the leg bones at the knee joint increases.

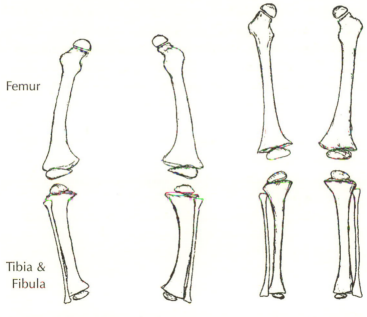

Femur

Tibia & Fibula

18 months   5 years

FIGURE 22. Development of the leg bones of a boy between the ages of eighteen months and five years. Notice the remarkable straightening of the leg bones. The disks at the ends of the bones—epiphyses—fuse with the shafts only after longitudinal growth ceases (around twenty years of age). (Author's drawings after x-ray pictures from Holt et al., 1954.)

Now, if the bones had continued to accommodate the stressing in this manner, the flaring would have worsened, the bones would have become heavier and more unwieldy, but at the same time the whole structure would have become more stable. Such legs would have been ungainly columns to stand on and difficult to move with. This, however, did not occur. Instead, the bones straightened and the flaring decreased, as the illustration shows. The legs became relatively light and straight columns. They lent stability, but also made movement possible.

In their form the legs follow the upright posture that the child has taken on and has been exercising for over three years. This indicates that not merely an accommodation to stresses is occurring, but in a certain sense stresses are being overcome by the tendency toward uprightness. We gain uprightness by counteracting what weighs us down. There is no uprightness in a world of weightlessness. The weight of the body both resists and stimulates our becoming upright. And in this interaction our body is formed.

Erwin Straus writes:

> Upright posture characterizes the human species. Nevertheless, each individual has to struggle in order to make it really his own. Man has to become what he is.... While the heart continues to beat from its fetal beginning to death without our active intervention and while breathing neither demands nor tolerates our voluntary interference beyond narrow limits, upright posture remains a task throughout our lives.... In getting up, in reaching the upright posture, man must oppose the forces of gravity. It seems to be his nature to oppose nature in its impersonal, fundamental aspects with natural means. However, gravity is

never fully overcome; upright posture always maintains
its character of counteraction. It calls for our activity
and attention. (Straus, 1966, p. 141)

This counteraction is present from the moment a child
initially brings itself to stand. We live in this willful process, overcoming the resistance of gravitational and
mechanical forces, which also include the resistance of
the not yet ideally formed body. The body is continuously
molded and remolded into a fine instrument for the activities that we carry out. It adapts to the way we stand and
move, becoming a reflection of the way we exist in the
world. Our body becomes ours.

We can thus begin to look through the body, as it were,
toward the individual. Imagine a young boy who, from the
time he begins to stand and walk, always stands and walks
on tiptoe. He continues to live in his body this way, and as
an adult he still usually walks and stands on tiptoe.
Already as a child he had unusually large calf muscles and
the front part of his feet were very wide. His body was
forming in accordance with his activity. It is a riddle why a
child takes on such a posture and gait. It results in a
unique way of relating to the body and to the world, but is
also a reflection of the will (I do not mean here a conscious process) to do so. If I awaken to the riddle of this
phenomenon, then it points beyond itself to the unique
individuality of this person.

The Environment of the Individual

The conditions for the development of the individual
lie not only within the self and the body, and not only
within the physical environment, but also within other
human beings. The environment that the child relates to

is essentially a human environment. One can argue about whether or not standing upright is due to imitation, but the fact is that this act always occurs in the context of standing and walking human beings who relate to the child. But this is not enough.

René Spitz describes children who were placed in an orphanage at birth (Spitz, 1965; for other case studies see Hassenstein, 1980). Their mothers, or other mothers, nursed the children during the first three months of life. Then the mothers left. Spitz reports that the food, hygiene, and medical treatment were as good or better than he had observed in other institutions. But one nurse was responsible for eight to twelve children at a time, with minimal contact occurring between the children and the nurses. Moreover, each child was cared for by more than one nurse per day and by a variety of nurses during the week.

When Spitz and his coworkers arrived at the orphanage, not one child had a toy. (From that point on the researchers themselves brought in toys.) To maintain peace and quiet, the nurses put blankets over the sides of the cribs, so that the children could see only the ceiling.

Within the first three months after their mothers' departure, the children's development was deeply disturbed. They cried frequently and were very demanding. Then they began to lose weight, with crying often giving way to screaming. Now the children *refused* the contact they had previously sought. They lay on their bellies in bed, began to suffer insomnia, and continued to lose weight. They became more susceptible to infectious diseases. Their movements slowed and their facial expressions grew rigid. Crying became whimpering.

After three months the children were completely passive. They were now lying on their backs and could not turn over. Their gaze was empty and their eye coordination deteriorated.

Of the ninety-one children Spitz observed, twenty-seven were dead at the end of the first year. He followed, at longer intervals, the development of the surviving children for four years. With few exceptions, none of the four-year-olds could sit, stand, walk, or talk. This utter tragedy occurred in an orphanage in the United States in the 1940s.

Spitz had studied another home for children, where similar symptoms had arisen, but in a milder form. There, too, symptoms set in when the mothers left, but in contrast to the first orphanage, the mothers often returned, whereupon the children usually recovered fairly quickly. It became evident that the continuity of care by one loving person is essential not only for emotional, but also for physical development.

Clearly, the individual without is necessary for the individual within to flourish.

Once Again, We and Our Genes

We can readily see that it is no simple matter to speak of heredity in the human being. Heredity does not thrust itself upon us like an object. Every organ, every characteristic, develops within a spectrum of influences ranging from gravitational and mechanical forces to human individuality. What is inherited in this dynamic process is invisible, and can be discerned only in thought. It is not static, but appears rather like a flexible model that is molded in the course of development. It is the living basis of all development.

The process is quite otherwise when we look for specific hereditary characteristics, whether the father's nose that we see in his children, or, more rigorously, the hereditarily conditioned disorder that has a specific family history, allowing it to be seen in Mendelian terms. Here we focus on particular traits. McKusick's catalog, *Mendelian Inheritance in Man,* lists all characteristics known or surmised to follow a Mendelian pattern. The 1986 edition includes some 3,900 traits, almost all of them heredity disorders. Mendelian inheritance is found only when something is discovered that is clearly distinguishable and separable from the norm. One might have expected the list to include "super-normal" traits just as frequently as disorders, but this is not the case. Mendelian traits have to do with limitations—extremes that inhibit or prohibit healthy functioning. When such disorders are recognized, the contrasting vitality of healthy states and processes becomes more tangible to the mind's eye.

When a gene is correlated with a disturbance of normal development, we conclude that the "normal" gene allows normal functioning. But this does not mean that the gene *causes* normal functioning. If a door swells and jams, it limits our movement. The normal door does not; but it also does not produce our movement, even if it channels it. Similarly, genes appear to be necessary, but not sufficient, conditions for physiological functions. All the genes in the genome taken together in any combination will not evoke the human being, or any other organism.

"Humans have (a few) genes, different from those of any other animal, giving our species the ability to 'change the world'" (Love, 1991). "Genetically, that is, in terms of information content, humans are 99% identical to chimpanzees. Indeed, argues Jared Diamond, a visitor from outer space would classify humans as a third species of chimpanzee, not with the separate classification that we award ourselves" (O'Neill et al., 1994).

These remarks suggest that the unique characteristics of the human being arise from a few genes. This quantitative view is not new. I am reminded of the debate concerning the premaxillary bone. This bone forms the front part of the muzzle in the upper jaw of mammals, but most anatomists of the eighteenth century agreed that it is not present in human beings. The premaxillary bone was like the last anatomical bastion of our humanity, separating us from the lower beasts. Goethe set out to find the bone in the human skull, and he succeeded (Goethe, 1988, pp. 111–116).

Convinced of the unity of mammalian organization, Goethe believed that the bone must be present at least in a germinal state in humans. He knew that our humanity is not something additive, to be indicated by the presence or absence of a bone, but a quality that informs every detail. This is exactly what we have seen in the study of the legs and feet. We come to a knowledge of human characteristics by attending to *how* the parts are formed in the whole. The unifying elements gel in our thinking; it is not a matter of fixed genetic traits correlated with fixed causal structures.

We cannot find our humanity in our genes. But because of the increasing progress in genetic diagnostics and manipulation, we will increasingly confront genetic questions and problems that *challenge* our humanity.

Gene Therapy

Gene therapies fall into two categories. In somatic gene therapy, genetic material is introduced into specific viruses or body cells (but not the germ, or reproductive, cells), which are then injected into the patient in the hope that the manipulated cells will function in a desired

way. Germ-line therapy, on the other hand, entails manipulating the fertilized egg or the reproductive cells des-
tined for fertilization.

Somatic Gene Therapy

The first approved attempt at somatic gene therapy
began in 1990. Researchers at the National Institutes of
Health (NIH) received permission to inject genetically
engineered cells into two girls, aged four and nine. The
girls suffered from adenosine deaminase (ADA) deficiency, a very rare form of immune deficiency (less than
one hundred people are affected worldwide) in which the
body has virtually no defenses against infections. What
would normally be a harmless, passing infection can lead
to death. ADA is an enzyme necessary for normal immune
reactions and is produced by white blood cells.

These two girls were receiving weekly injections of an
encapsulated form of the ADA enzyme derived from cows.
The drug improved their condition, but their immune
responses were still weak. Therefore, the NIH researchers
attempted gene therapy (Blaese et al., 1995).

They removed white blood cells from the girls. The cells
were kept alive in laboratory cultures. They then added a
genetically altered virus to the culture of white blood cells.
These viruses contained the DNA necessary for ADA synthesis. As in other experiments, only a small percentage of
cells took up the viruses, but when these divided, a clone
of genetically engineered white blood cells with the ADA
DNA was formed.

These cultured cells were then reinfused into the girls'
bloodstream, in hopes that some of the genetically engineered cells would produce ADA. One girl received eleven
infusions and the other twelve over the course of two years.

In one girl the ADA enzyme activity increased signifi-
cantly. As an indication of her improved immune
response, the number of lymphocytes (T cells, a type of
cell that interacts with B cells; the latter make antibodies)
rose and stabilized at a normal level within six months.
The infusions were stopped after two years, and in the
three years since then the enzyme activity has remained.

The other girl's reactions to the therapy were much
more ambiguous. Her T-cell count rose rapidly after the
first infusions, but then dropped off to levels comparable
to those before the therapy began. In addition, ADA
enzyme activity did not increase. But other immune reactions improved—her lymph nodes and tonsils grew and
became visible, as they had in the first girl.

The differences in the case histories of these two girls
show clearly the need to consider therapy in light of the
individual. One cannot expect uniformly successful results.

The researchers view the case of the one girl as clear evidence of the efficacy of gene therapy. The interpretation of
the girl's increasing health remains problematic, however,
because she was also receiving the ADA-enzyme as a thera-
peutic agent during the whole course of gene therapy.

Gene therapy has received a good deal of attention in
the media, and by the fall of 1995 there had been over one
hundred clinical trials with almost six hundred patients.
Little has been published about these trials, and the results
on the whole have been disappointing (Marshall, 1995a,
Coghlan, 1995). For example, an attempt to help twelve
patients with cystic fibrosis by transferring DNA to their
nasal epithelium in hopes of normalizing secretion had no
positive effect. In fact, when higher doses of the DNA-car-
rying virus were administered in three patients, two
reacted with strong inflammations (Knowles et al., 1995).

As one researcher, Inda Vermer, stated in 1992, "The idea of doing gene therapy is now more acceptable. I don't know why. It is not the success of experiments" (quoted in Thompson, 1992). The prospect of economic gain is certainly one factor. Private companies fund 60% of all gene therapy trials, and scientists and doctors doing research often have a stake in genetic engineering companies. "This trend is worrying some leaders in the field, who say biotech companies are forcing the pace and direction of research, and not always in ways anchored in the best science" (Marshall, 1995a).

In December 1995, an NIH panel—NIH spends about $200 million per year on gene therapy research—released a report stating that gene therapy is being clearly oversold by its proponents and backers. It points to the mere "anecdotal claims of successful therapy" and to the fact that even in animal experiments there has been no success in curing an illness. The report emphasizes the need for more thorough research—"less hype, more biology," as the title of an article in *Science* expressed it (Marshall, 1995b).

Germ-line Therapy

Germ-line therapy for humans is still off limits. Any successfully effected changes would be hereditary, which is not—at least according to present knowledge and theories—the case with somatic gene therapy. Germ-line therapy in human beings would entail operations like those producing transgenic mice, as described in chapter 5. It is technically feasible to perform such experiments with human eggs and embryos today.

Why isn't it done? On the one hand, most people still consider such manipulations morally reprehensible. On the other hand, the techniques are not reliable enough. As

I have pointed out, the work with animals yields only about a 1% success rate, and the results are not predictable. The likelihood of undesired effects is so great that such experiments on human beings would be considered irresponsible even from the narrow standpoint afforded by current animal experimentation.

Will further technical improvements influence the strong moral inhibitions currently prevailing? I believe that the more exact and predictable the experiments become, the more willing scientists and doctors will be to work on human eggs and embryos. This progress will put our conceptions of the human being to the test. Suzuki and Knudtson rightly point out:

> The fact is that almost any scientific advance that grants greater access to human reproductive cells and embryos hastens the day when the genetic manipulation of human germ cells will become medically feasible. Each new breakthrough in human reproductive technology, in a sense, draws the human egg, sperm and embryo one step farther out of the dark, protective sanctuary of the womb and into the bright light of future genetic control. (Suzuki and Knudtson, 1990, pp. 186ff)

Genetic Diagnosis

Genetic diagnosis can be prenatal or postnatal, and entails the isolation of genetic structures and substances (chromosomes and DNA) correlated with specific traits. Prenatal diagnosis is used almost exclusively to gain information about hereditary diseases or disorders. This is also true of one aspect of postnatal diagnosis, which is often termed "genetic screening." In both cases we have to do with prognoses and not diagnoses, since there are no symptoms unless one considers genetic structures them-selves to be symptoms. With known disorders, the isolation and identification of the genetic structures leads to a prog-nosis of what may follow.

Diagnosis also finds use in forensic science. Just as each individual's fingerprint is unique, it is assumed that each individual's DNA is unique, constituting a "DNA finger-print." If one analyzes the DNA from a blood spot or piece of hair at a crime scene, and if it is interpreted as matching the DNA of the suspect, the correlation may become the basis for a conviction. This method appears at first view straightforward, but in fact it is not accepted as reliable by all experts—particularly in the way results are interpreted (cf. Lewontin and Hartl, 1991, and Lander, 1989).

Preimplantation Diagnosis

There has been rapid progress in identifying genes related to specific disorders and diseases. At the same time, ever earlier diagnosis has become possible. Amniocentesis allows the analysis of fetal chromosomes and DNA between the fourteenth and twenty-first weeks of pregnancy. Chorion villi biopsy reaches back to the seventh week of pregnancy. Within the past few years it has become possible to perform so-called preimplantation diagnosis. To indicate how far researchers and doctors proceed today, I will describe this procedure in more detail in a particular case.

Cystic fibrosis is a potentially fatal disease characterized by thickened secretions in organs like the lungs and pan-creas, which can lead to insufficiency of these organs and death. It is one of the most common hereditarily condi-tioned diseases that follow a Mendelian pattern. Through studying family history, it is possible to determine the like-lihood of a couple giving birth to an affected child.

This particular case concerns three English couples, each already having had at least one child with cystic fibrosis (Handyside et al., 1992). The couples wanted more children, but they "wished to minimize the risk of termination of pregnancy affected by cystic fibrosis"—that is, they wished to avoid abortion. Handyside et al. offered these couples the alternative of in vitro fertilization combined with preimplantation diagnosis. The procedure was as follows.

The women were treated with hormones to stimulate the ovulation of many eggs at one time. The eggs were then removed and inseminated with the husband's sperm. Of the thirty-seven eggs removed, fourteen fertilized normally. Thirteen of the embryos that developed from these eggs were then subjected to preimplantation diagnosis.

After fertilization, the egg begins to divide into cells—first two, then four, then eight, and so on. This process is called cleavage and can occur outside the body in an appropriate medium. The embryo is spherical with a diameter of 0.1 mm (the size of the tip of a needle) and is enclosed in a membrane called the zona pellucida. In the case under consideration, on the third day after fertilization, when the embryos contained four or eight cells, the researchers created a hole in the zona pellucida with a fine stream of acidic medium. Inserting a tiny micropipette (inner diameter: 0.03 mm) into the embryo, they gently sucked out a single cell.

The embryos were now lacking one cell, which the researchers assumed—primarily on the basis of experiments with mammals such as mice—would have no adverse effect. During the ensuing eight hours each cell was genetically analyzed for DNA specifically associated with cystic fibrosis. This is a complicated procedure and a remarkable technical feat. A major problem is that only a minute amount of DNA can be isolated from a single cell, too little to be analyzed. However, an ingenious method called *polymerase chain reaction* (PCR) was used to amplify the DNA to produce a sufficient amount for genetic analysis. The DNA was then heated to allow it to bind to other DNA. A portion of the amplified DNA from the embryo was mixed with DNA taken and amplified from cells of healthy individuals ("normal DNA"), and another portion was mixed with DNA taken and amplified from cells of individuals suffering from cystic fibrosis ("cystic fibrosis DNA"). These mixtures were subjected to gel electrophoresis, and the resulting bands indicated whether the embryo's DNA had bound to the normal DNA, to the cystic fibrosis DNA, or to both.

The researchers could then conclude that the embryo had contained zero, one, or two copies of the cystic fibrosis gene. If the embryo's DNA bound only to normal DNA, then the prognosis was that it would not suffer from cystic fibrosis. If its DNA bound to both types of DNA, then it was diagnosed as a "carrier," meaning its cells have normal DNA to compensate for the effects of the cystic fibrosis DNA. Finally, if its DNA bound only to the cystic fibrosis DNA, then the prognosis was that the person developing out of the embryo would in all likelihood later suffer from cystic fibrosis.

In the latter case, the embryo was "discarded." (This is the term conventionally used.) Five embryos were discarded in all. The diagnosis of one woman's nondiscarded embryos was not successful, so none of her embryos could be considered for transfer into her womb. Some embryos of the other women were diagnosed as having no copies of the cystic fibrosis gene or as being carriers, and these were considered for transfer. These couples chose to have one carrier and one "normal" embryo transferred. (It is common practice to transfer two embryos, so that there is a greater likelihood that at least one will implant and develop further. The probability of having twins, of course, also increases.)

After the embryos were transferred into the mothers, one could only wait and see how nature took her course. Only one of the women became pregnant, and she with one child. She gave birth to a healthy girl whose cells were determined to be free of the cystic fibrosis gene.

The Human Being As an Object of Genetic Biotechnology

With genetic technologies we seize hold of fate, destiny, luck, chance—whatever we prefer to call those previously inaccessible natural workings that strongly influence the course of our lives. Choices arise, and we have to make decisions. The crucial question is whether we will consciously accept responsibility for our decisions, or instead sleep through the call for awakening.

The awakening is much less likely once we have convinced ourselves by all our methods and thoughts that we are manipulating *objects*. As human beings we indeed have an object aspect, but I hope to have shown clearly enough in the course of this work that our humanity as such cannot be captured with object categories. The difficulty facing us is that we must try to bring a conscious exercise of responsibility precisely to those spheres in which we can effectively manipulate things, but at the same time our activity in these spheres invites us to treat human life ever more as a mere object.

Let us look at the objectification process more closely. In the example of preimplantation diagnosis, the eggs were removed from the body, the sperm fertilized them in a petri dish, the first stages of development occurred there, and the embryo underwent, as it were, an operation. Unfit embryos were discarded. This last deed embodied the judgment, "Such embryos are dispensable objects."

In most countries experiments on embryos—which end in their being discarded—are allowed up to fourteen days after fertilization. A notable exception is Germany, where the burden of the Nazi eugenic practices lives on as conscience. When, in 1990, a law was passed in Germany forbidding embryo research, the journal *Nature* reported the decision in a brief article entitled "Embryo research: Germany turns back clock" (Dickman, 1990).

This same issue of the journal brought an article by Handyside et al. (1990) to unprecedentedly rapid publication, so that it could affect a decision by the British House of Commons concerning embryo research. The article dealt with preimplantation diagnosis. (While most *Nature* articles are published a number of months after submission, this one appeared two days after.)

I mention these two examples to illustrate how strong the interests are behind such research.

Some researchers may convince themselves that an objective force compels their work, removing it from the realm of choice. The necessity of embryo research is clearly stated by Robert Edwards, who developed some of the techniques for in vitro fertilization:

I clearly remember the day, a year or so later, when I sat with Patrick [Steptoe].... We were both enormously excited, for we had just seen for ourselves through a

microscope four beautiful human blastocysts [the
stage of the embryo before implantation], the first
ever grown in culture. They seemed outwardly perfect,
but we had yet to be certain of their inner structure.

"What are we going to do with them?" Patrick asked.

"We're going to flatten them, to check their chromosomes," I replied.

"So what do I tell my patients?" Patrick insisted.

"I've got to see that the cell nuclei and the chromosomes are good," I said. "We will be able to explain to
them that we have taken another step forward."

Was this the right decision? The right decision for
Patrick's patients, or the right decision for science? It
was a fair decision, but another might have been better. Those blastocysts could have been replaced in
their mother's womb rather than used as research
material. But then, imagine the public outcry if, as a
result of my not checking their nuclei and chromosomes, the first child born of IVF had been defective!
Our work would have been stopped dead. Without
research on those early embryos there would have
been no test-tube babies for the infertile, not even
now, twenty years later.

It must be said ... that embryo research often results
in the destruction of these microscopic living organisms. An embryo removed from its culture fluid dies
very quickly. Many kinds of in-vitro examination also
damage embryos so that they no longer develop.
Embryos that are either dead or seriously deformed
are destroyed: incinerated with other laboratory waste
as often as not. Some of these, if returned carefully to a
woman's womb, might possibly have developed into
human beings, possibly into malformed human

beings. There are rights and wrongs to this, and I will discuss them later.... Undeniably, research on human embryos is still desperately needed. (Edwards, 1989, pp. 71ff.)

Edwards' candid description is revealing. First, he chooses to perform in vitro fertilization, the result of which is that some embryos begin to develop. Now he has the opportunity to transfer such embryos into their mother's womb, but this requires knowing whether the embryos are healthy. Therefore he "must" perform experiments. This is all very logical, but it glosses over the fact that there is no necessity except the necessity the researcher chooses to bind himself with.

By objectifying our actions, we begin to abandon responsibility for personal choices. We begin to believe that the processes in which we participate are governed only by external forces. That is, we forget ourselves when we objectify, and an absent self cannot take responsibility for its actions.

The problem of objectification also shows up in discussions about when an embryo becomes human. There is no question that, biologically speaking, human life is present at every stage of development. And yet each stage is different and has its unique characteristics. Whether we try to define humanity at fertilization, implantation, the first heartbeat, the first brain activity, birth, adolescence, exercise of the right to vote, or the attainment of the wisdom of old age, we are undertaking a fruitless task because we are ignoring the fact that the human being is inherently a developing being. Any resulting definition will never do justice to an actual human life, whose being is expressed throughout the entire course of development.

Needless to say, a definition *can* serve a particular prejudice. If I want to perform experiments on embryos, it will be comforting to think of a preimplantation embryo as not yet human, just as I will prefer to deny humanity to the twelve-week-old fetus I want to abort. I am not here speaking abstractly or categorically against abortion, nor am I denying that our humanity manifests in different ways at different times in development. Rather, I am trying to dispel the comfortable cloud of delusion that prevents us from placing ourselves consciously and responsibly in the middle of the concrete life situation. Full-blooded reality flies in the face of fixed viewpoints.

Cloning Human Embryos

We have learned to see that there is an intimate connection between thinking and action. If I believe in an object-knowledge independent of my choices and attitudes as a knower, then ethics becomes an after-the-fact, separate problem. I perform experiments, gain a particular type of knowledge, and then ask afterward whether there are moral questions to address.

A case in point is the report on the cloning of preimplantation embryos. The idea of cloning human embryos is by no means new, and has been the subject of much discussion and speculation. But only recently has it become technically possible (Kolberg, 1993).

The technique was developed and carried out by Jerry Hall, the director of the In Vitro Fertilization and Andrology Laboratory at George Washington University. Hall and his colleagues took seventeen embryos in the two- to eight-cell stage following in vitro fertilization. These had developed from eggs penetrated by more than one sperm and were therefore considered unfit for transfer into their mothers. Since the embryos were to be discarded, the researchers saw no reason not to experiment with them first. They separated the individual cells of each embryo and coated them with an artificial zona pellucida. In a nutrient medium a total of forty-eight new embryos developed, some up to the thirty-two-cell stage. This means that each of the seventeen original embryos gave rise to an average of three genetically identical embryos. Theoretically, each set could have developed into "identical triplets."

Why did Hall perform the experiments? On the one hand, "we were just answering a basic research question"—that is, seeing whether the cloning technique would work. On the other hand, Hall was quite aware that cloning human embryos is a volatile issue. But "it was clear that it was a matter of time until someone was going to do it, and we decided it would be better for us to do it in an open manner and get the ethical discussion going" (quoted in Kolberg, 1993).

Hall is certainly correct in believing that what he calls the ethical discussion would not get moving until something was actually *done*, after the fact. Then we wake up a little. But this is not being awake to the doing itself, which includes from the outset an ethical component and a series of choices.

Outer Pressures and Inner Uprightness

Earlier we heard Edwards say that embryo experimentation is necessary in order to improve in vitro fertilization techniques. He also described why parents want to have children—even if through in vitro fertilization—which in turn influences him to perform and perfect the procedure:

Clearly the cultural pressures on men and women to reproduce are enormous. "There is a long-standing Christian concern that marriage, whenever possible, should lead to parenthood," wrote a board set up by the Church of England to study the matter in 1985. On a secular level, too, the pressures are wide-ranging. Laws of inheritance, the continuance of family name and position, the perceived roles of women as mothers and men as providers, the extensions of identity that children provide, the sense of purpose given by their rearing, the pride in their successes, the hope of their companionship and support in the parents' old age, even the promise they bring of grandchildren—the social expectations fulfilled by children are many and diverse.... There are pressures of custom, also: the community's broad assumption that childless couples are in some way diminished, failed, subjects for pity or even disapproval. And then, of course, there are economic pressures. In many areas—farming, for example, or privately-owned business—children are a parent's best hope of on-going prosperity, of land tenure or of commercial continuity.... More powerful still are genetic pressures.... But the fact undeniably remains that for very many men and women the deep genetic need exists for a child that is perceived to be in some immediate physical sense their own, *of their blood.* For such people, should they be infertile, adoption is no solution. (Edwards, 1989, pp. 25ff.)

The human being in this picture is determined from without, moved and infringed upon by outside pressures. Actions are only reactions. But we do not have to be passive; we can actively influence the pressures themselves—

some more, some less, and the situation is different for each individual. The individual in us develops in relation to—and in opposition to—these pressures. We develop individuality through struggling with them, which also means through struggling with ourselves. "We have the power not only to place the weights, but—if I may put it this way—*to be the weights* on the balance" (Herder, 1982, my translation). Remember the upright posture! The upright posture is both the deed of, and a picture for, individuality. Uprightness is not automatic; it is constantly being attained and modified. We must each find our own individual center of balance, and from this point of self-determination relate to ourselves and to the world.

I am pointing here to a specific quality, a quality of inner uprightness appropriate to individuality. It can live in every fiber of a process and imbue it with responsibility. I am not appealing to a fixed and particular norm that all should follow, for this would leave little opening for conscious development.

Taking Development Seriously

Up until the last few decades embryonic development and fetal development were a matter of an inward and bodily mediated relationship of the mother to her developing child. It did not have an object quality. Of course, one could look at books and videos with pictures of the developing embryo and fetus, but such pictures did not coincide with the inner experience of the pregnancy.

Prenatal diagnosis does not deal with "general human development," but with *my* child. It is in this sense concrete. But if a "negative" diagnosis is given, something strange can happen. The inner relationship can completely change because the parents cease imagining *their child* in his or her own right, and instead begin imagining an objectified *illness* or *syndrome.*

Normally we consider the human embryo or fetus as full of potential. It bears a future, we look forward, there is uncertainty and expectancy. The moment an abnormal genetic diagnosis is given, there is the greatest danger that this picture dies into a predetermined, fixed destiny. We picture the malformed, abnormal child who is doomed to idiocy, a child who will be a burden for us and society. We have, in our imaginations, already killed the child without the use of physical instruments.

I hope you will excuse this drastic expression, but it is accurate. Through prenatal diagnosis we may label a child in such a way that it becomes an abnormal object determined solely by its inheritance. Our mental picture of the child is dead, and to abort in this case is simply to carry out physically what is already the meaning of our thoughts.

This is the danger associated with a purely genetic consideration of the human being. It enshrines the past as a constricting factor determining present and future. Or, rather, present and future degenerate into a mere continuation of the past. This is why the concept of genetic screening for insurance and hiring is inhuman. Decisions not to hire or insure on the basis of a genetic diagnosis (which is, by way of reminder, a *prognosis*) would clearly be discriminatory. Fortunately, the National Institutes of Health (Department of Energy Working Group on Ethical, Legal and Social Implications of the Human Genome Project) has come to a similar conclusion:

> Meaningful protection against genetic discrimination requires that insurers be prohibited from using all information about genes, gene products, or inherited

characteristics to deny or limit health insurance cover-
age. (Hudson et al., 1995)

Imagine yourself as a healthy thirty-year-old. Your father
died of Huntington's disease, a degenerative disease of the
central nervous system. This disease follows a Mendelian
dominant pattern. Children are seldom affected; more
commonly the symptoms appear around forty or fifty years
of age, worsen over the next ten to fifteen years, and finally
lead to death. There is no cure. As a healthy thirty-year-old
you know you may carry the Huntington's disease gene.
You undergo a genetic test that indicates you are in fact a
carrier. Now, you may ask, "Am I really healthy, or do I
'have' the disease and only *feel* healthy?"

When we mistake genetic diagnosis for a medical diagnosis, we run the danger of picturing a clear-cut, fixed destiny. The genetic diagnosis gives ground only for a general
prognosis that the disease *may* occur. Everything else is
open—you may even die of other natural causes before
symptoms of Huntington's appear. One can imagine the
catastrophic consequences when a child "knows" that its
genetic destiny will be fulfilled when it later in life comes
down with Huntington's disease.

At the beginning of this chapter we looked at the rich
and complex context in which the flexible inherited
potential is embedded. Identifying a Mendelian or other
disorder means identifying particular limitations in a
human being's development. But we must not forget that
the reality of the individual child will be different from any
abstract picture we form. We tend simply to forget development when we think in static, genetic terms. The birth of a
child, whether "normal" or "abnormal," calls forth massive
changes in the environment into which it is born. Through

its presence the parents and siblings change, and this in turn is reflected in the way they interact with the child. It is a living process. A diseased, retarded, or malformed child may even mobilize more of the truly human forces in its environment, because it is so needy.

Clearly, parents must form their own picture of the coming child. But it is also clear that their picture will be influenced by those considered expert. When Edwards calls Down's Syndrome a "disastrous inheritance" (Edwards, 1989, p. 53), it is his genetic book knowledge speaking. What counts in that context is the abnormal chromosome configuration associated with a list of abnormal traits. Imagine a woman or couple being counseled by Edwards concerning a fetus diagnosed with Down's Syndrome. Wouldn't they want to avoid "disaster" and abort the fetus? But has Edwards ever experienced a child with Down's Syndrome? Does his restricted viewpoint as an expert actually prevent him from being a competent advisor?

Here is another response to such children:

> Their puckish nature has been remarked on by all who work with them. Lively, cheerful, and very affectionate, Down syndrome patients are noted for their impishness, flair for mimicry, and enjoyment of music and dance. (Mange and Mange, 1980, p. 120)

We can see here the great responsibility accepted by genetic counselors. Do they strive for a comprehensive yet open picture that surveys the possibility of development by all individuals involved?

The handicapped or retarded individual is, unfortunately, highly susceptible to being treated according to an impersonal scheme. The outer limitation looms so strongly that we tend to forget what we presuppose in all other human beings: the unique individual. The handicapped person has a handicap, but he or she is not the handicap. Just as, in considering foot and bone structure, we looked through the body toward the individual, so we must look through the handicap.

Every disability, retardation, or handicap presents a challenge to our concept of the individual. And the more courage and uprightness we develop as individuals, the more the individual in the other will find space to develop.

CONCLUSION

Thinking "inflicts the wound, but also heals it" (Hegel, 1977, p. 88, my translation). When we question and think about the world, we are separated from it. At the same time, through questioning and thinking we also begin to overcome separation. Every moment of understanding forges a connection with the world.

Geneticists view organisms in terms of discrete traits and genes. The organism is considered as an effect of the workings of its interacting parts. This approach leads to the conclusion that the same substances and mechanisms determine heredity in all organisms—bacteria, tobacco plants, fruit flies, mice, and human beings. The resulting genetic pictures are clear and convincing.

But there is a problem inherent in the intellect's way of coming to knowledge. Emerson alludes to it when he writes:

> Intellect separates the fact considered from you, from all local and personal reference, and it discerns it as if it existed for its own sake.... But a truth, separated by the intellect, is no longer a subject of destiny. We hold it as a god upraised above care and fear. And so any fact in our life, ... disentangled from the web of our

unconsciousness, becomes an object impersonal and
immortal. It is the past restored, but embalmed.
(Emerson, 1950, pp. 292–293)

When we gain clarity through the intellect, we establish
a new relation to the object of our understanding. And
yet, since we are focused on a narrow fact or truth, we
ignore our own activity along with the context out of
which we have abstracted the fact. In this sense, all intellectual activity—to use Hegel's image—continually inflicts
new wounds. It creates separation. This is the dilemma of
science.

We can help to heal the wounds when we go beyond
viewing the phenomena—ourselves included—as separate
objects. We can restore the context our intellect has here-
tofore ignored. We come to know the organism in its environment by discovering a fabric of relationships in which
we, too, participate. Neither organism nor environment
can be understood without the other. Moreover, each
organism along with its environment presents us with a
new context, a new challenge to the flexibility of our
minds. Perhaps the greatest hurdle is to rethink the gene,
to begin to see it as part of a living organism.

How we think determines what kinds of connections we
make with the world through our actions. Our actions
precipitate out of our thinking, and the results and effects
of these deeds carry the signature of our minds. The history of genetics shows this, and future developments in
genetics and genetic engineering will continue to do so.
The visage of our landscapes already carries the imprint
of human culture and technology. Increasingly, by means
of genetic manipulation, organisms themselves will bear
our hereditarily anchored stamp.

It becomes eminently important, therefore, to examine the way we have chosen, or been taught, to grasp the world. This is the only means of establishing a conscious connection with the effects of our actions. It is the basis for taking responsibility.

A contextual approach is not to be looked at as yet another solidified doctrine or theory. Rather, it is a necessary complement to the prevailing conceptions and practices of contemporary science. It is a way of making science a healthier whole, modeled after the organisms it studies.

GLOSSARY

I have kept to a minimum the number of technical terms used in this book. Where technical terms could not be avoided, I have tried to describe and explain the concepts in their relevant context, therefore I refer the reader to the index. The definitions below, lacking their context, can serve only for quick reference. This is especially the case for concepts like *DNA* or *gene*, which are developed throughout the book.

Amino acids. The products of protein analysis; conversely, proteins are synthesized in the cells of organisms out of a total of 20 different amino acids.

Amniocentesis. A procedure to remove fetal cells from the amniotic fluid that surrounds the fetus. The cells are used for genetic analysis.

Blastocyst. An early stage in the development of the mammalian embryo, before it implants into the womb.

Chorion villi biopsy. A procedure to remove fetal tissue from the chorion villi for genetic analysis. The chorion is a precursor of the placenta; the villi are small finger-like projections of the chorion.

Chromosomes. Rod-shaped bodies that can be observed under a microscope in cells during cell division. They form out of the cell nucleus. The chemical analysis of chromosomes results in different substances: deoxyribonucleic acid, ribonucleic acid, and proteins.

Clone. 1) A group of cells that have descended from one parent cell. 2) Genetically identical organisms that have descended from one parent organism via asexual reproduction. 3) Identical sequences of DNA (genes) that have been produced by bacteria, or other organisms.

Deoxyribonucleic acid (DNA). Substance that can be isolated out of the nucleus of cells, bacterial chromosomes, and most viruses. It has been identified as the primary genetic material.

Enzymes. Proteins that catalyze metabolic processes in organisms.

Gel electrophoresis. Analytical tool to separate substances from each other by having them move on a gel through an electrically charged field.

Gene. In Mendelian genetics, the theoretical unit of heredity applied to interpret the inheritance of traits. In modern genetics conceived to be a functional segment of DNA associated with the synthesis of a protein (or polypeptide).

Genome. Concept used to describe the totality of genes within a cell or an organism, depending on the context.

Germ cells. Reproductive cells: sperm and egg.

Germ line. Those cells that become differentiated from the rest of the developing organism's cells and that then form the germ cells.

Homologous pair. Refers to two identical chromosomes in a cell.

Hybrid. In narrow terms, the progeny of a cross between two varieties or races of the same species, which themselves have been produced by repeated self-fertilization or inbreeding. More generally, the progeny of a cross between parents of different genetic types or different species.

Implantation. Process in which the young embryo (blastocyst) grows into the lining of the uterus.

Mutation. A change in the amount, order, or structure of genetic material in a cell or virus.

Polypeptide. A protein or part of a protein, composed of amino acids.

Proteins. Essential substances in all organisms, both structurally and functionally (for example, as enzymes). Proteins are synthesized out of amino acids.

Replication. In genetics refers to the process through which exact copies of DNA are produced in cells and viruses.

Ribonucleic acid (RNA). Functionally essential in the synthesis of proteins. In some viruses (retroviruses) it functions, instead of DNA, as genetic material.

T Cells (synonymous with T Lymphocytes). They are important components of the immune system; some stimulate the maturation of the antibody-producing B cells, while others destroy infected cells.

Trait. In genetic terms, a feature of an organism viewed as a clearly defined, hereditarily stable characteristic.

Transgenic. Refers to an organism that has been genetically manipulated at the outset of its development and then carries foreign genes in all or most of its body's cells.

Zona pellucida. The membrane surrounding the egg of mammals.

Zygote. The fertilized egg.

REFERENCES

Anthony, C., and N. Kolthoff. 1975. *Anatomy and physiology.* St. Louis: C. V. Mosby Company.

Avery, O. T. et al. 1944. Studies on the chemical nature of the substance inducing transformation of pneumococcal types. *J. of Experimental Medicine* 79:137–158.

Bacon, F. 1980. *Francis Bacon: a selection of his works.* Ed. Sidney Warhaft. Indianapolis: The Odyssey Press.

Barfield, O. 1965. *Saving the appearances.* New York: Harcourt, Brace and World, Inc.

Barfield, O. 1973. *Poetic diction.* Middletown, Conn.: Wesleyan University Press.

Bearn, A. G., and J. L. German. 1961. Chromosomes and disease. *Scientific American* 205:66–76.

Bennett, A. et al. 1990. Rapid evolution in response to high-temperature selection. *Nature* 346:79–81.

Benninghof, A., and K. Goerttler. 1980. *Lehrbuch der Anatomie des Menschen,* Band I. 13th ed. Munich: Urban & Schwarzenberg.

Bialy, H. 1991. Transgenic pharming comes of age. *Bio/Technology* 9:786–788.

Blaese, R. M. et al. 1995. T lymphocyte-directed gene therapy for ADA⁻ SCID: Initial trial results after 4 years. *Science* 270:475–480.

Bockemühl, J. 1969. Gartenkresse, Kamille, Baldrian: Eine neue Methode, das Wurzelwachstum in der Erde im Verhältnis zur oberirdischen Entwicklung der Pflanze zu beobachten. *Elemente der Naturwissenschaft* 11:13–28.

Bockemühl, J. 1972. Der Jahreslauf als Ganzheit in der Natur. *Elemente der Naturwissenschaft* 16:17–33.

Bockemühl, J. 1981. *In partnership with nature.* Kimberton, Pa.: Bio-Dynamic Literature.

Bockemühl, J. 1992. *Awakening to landscape.* Dornach, Switzerland: Natural Science Section, Goetheanum, Dornach, Switzerland (Distr. by Anthroposophic Press, Hudson, N.Y.).

Braenden, C., and T. Jones. 1990. Between objectivity and subjectivity. *Nature* 343:687–89.

Chambon, P. 1981. Split genes. *Scientific American* 244:48–59.

Coghlan, A. 1995. Gene dream fades away. *New Scientist* 25 November: 14–15.

Cohen, S. N. 1975. The manipulation of genes. *Scientific American* 233:24–33.

Cohen, S. N. et al. 1973. Construction of biologically functional bacterial plasmids *in vitro. Proc. Nat. Acad. Sci.* 70:3240–3244.

Cohen, S. N., and J. A. Shapiro. 1980. Transposable genetic elements. *Scientific American* 242:40–49.

Commoner, B. 1968. Failure of the Watson-Crick theory as a chemical explanation of inheritance. *Nature* 220:334–340.

Crick, F. 1970. Central dogma of molecular biology. *Nature* 227: 561–563.

Davies, K. 1992. Mulling over mouse models. *Nature* 359:86.

Dickman, S. 1990. Embryo research: Germany turns back clock. *Nature* 348:8.

Dixon, B. 1992. Surprise is research's reprise. *Bio/Technology* 10:111.

Dykhuizen, D. 1990. Mountaineering with microbes. *Nature* 346:15–16.

Edelglass, S. et al. 1992. *Matter and mind.* Hudson N.Y.: Lindisfarne Press.

Edwards, R. 1989. *Life before birth.* London: Hutchinson.

Emerson, R. W. 1950. Intellect. In *The complete essays and other writings of Ralph Waldo Emerson.* New York: The Modern Library (Random House).

Fischer, E. 1991. *Die Beweglichkeit der Gene.* Germany: Goldmann Verlag.

Gilbert, W. 1991. Towards a paradigm shift in biology. *Nature* 349:99.

Goethe, J. W. 1977. *Schriften zur Naturwissenschaft.* Ed. Michael Boehler. Reclam: Stuttgart.

Goethe, J. W. 1988. *Scientific studies.* Ed. Douglas Miller. Suhrkamp, New York.

Goode, A. W., and P. C. Rambaut. 1985. The skeleton in space. *Nature* 317:204–205.

Greene, A., and R. Allison. 1994. Recombination between viral RNA and transgenic plant transcripts. *Science* 263:1423–1425.

Groh, T., and S. McFadden. 1990. *Farms of tomorrow.* Kimberton, PA.: Biodynamic Farming & Gardening Assoc.

Haeckel, E. 1866. *Generelle Morphologie der Organismen,* Bd. I. Berlin: Georg Reimer.

Handyside, A. H. et al. 1990. Pregnancies from biopsied human pre-implantation embryos sexed by Y-specific DNA amplification. *Nature* 344:768–770.

Handyside, A.H. et al. 1992. Birth of a normal girl after in vitro fertilization and preimplantation diagnostic testing for cystic fibrosis. *The New England Journal of Medicine* 327:905–909.

Harlow, E. 1992. For our eyes only. *Nature* 359:270–271.

Hassenstein, B. 1980. *Verhaltensbiologie des Kindes.* Munich: R. Piper & Co. Verlag .

Hegel, G. W. F. 1977. *Enzyklopädie der philosophischen Wissenschaften,* Werke, Bd. 8, Teil 1. Frankfurt am Main: Suhrkamp Verlag.

Herder, J. G. 1982. *Ideen zur Philosophie der Geschichte der Menschheit,* vierter Band, p. 65. Berlin: Aufbauverlag.

Holdrege, C. 1986. Schritte zur Bildung eines lebendigen Vererbungsbegriffes. *Elemente der Naturwissenschaft* 45:27–61.

Holt, J. F. et al. 1954. Physiological bowing of the legs in young children. *Journal of the American Medical Assoc.* 154:390–394.

Hsu, J. D. 1982. Skeletal changes in children with neuromuscular disorders. In *Factors and mechanisms influencing bone growth,* pp. 137–165. New York: Alan Liss Inc.

Hubbard, R. and E. Wald. 1993. *Exploding the gene myth.* Boston: Beacon Press.

Hudson, K. L. et al. 1995. Genetic discrimination and health insurance: an urgent need for reform. *Science* 270:391–393.

Jones, J. S. 1991. Songs in the key of life (review of three books). *Nature* 354:323.

Judson, H. 1979. *The eighth day of creation.* New York: Simon and Schuster.

Juskevich, J., and C.G. Guyer. 1990. Bovine growth hormone: human food safety evaluation. *Science* 249:875–884.

Kell, D. 1991. Lacuna seeker. *Nature* 350:268.

Keller, E. 1983. *A feeling for the organism.* New York: W. H. Freeman and Company.

Knowles, M. et al. 1995. A controlled study of adenoviral-vector-mediated gene transfer in the nasal epithelium of patients with cystic fibrosis. *The New England Journal of Medicine* 333:823–831.

Kolata, G. 1993a. Cystic fibrosis surprise: genetic screening falters. *New York Times* Nov. 16:C1.

Kolata, G. 1993b. Unlocking the secrets of the genome. *New York Times* Nov. 30:C1.

Kolberg, R. 1993. Human embryo cloning reported. *Science* 262:652–653.

Koopman, P. et al. 1991. Male development of chromosomally female mice transgenic for Sry. *Nature* 351:117–121.

Kranich, E. M. 1994. Das Rind—eine tierkundliche Betrachtung. *Erziehungskunst* 3:195–202.

Krimpenfort, P. et al. 1991. Generation of transgenic dairy cattle using "in vitro" embryo production. *Bio/Technology* 9:844–847.

Krumbiegel, I. 1967. *Gregor Mendel.* Stuttgart: Wissenschaftliche Verlagsgesellschaft.

Lamb, G. 1994. Community supported agriculture. *Threefold Review* 11:39–43.

Lander, E. S. 1989. DNA fingerprinting on trial. *Nature* 339:501–505.

Lander, E. S., and N. J. Schork. 1994. Genetic dissection of complex traits. *Science* 265:2037–2048.

Larson, R. L. 1973. Physical activity and the growth and development of bone and joint structures. In *Physical activity,* ed. G. L. Rarick. New York and London: Academic Press.

Lewontin, R. C. 1991. *Biology as ideology.* New York: Harper Perennial.

Lewontin, R. C., and D.L. Hartl. 1991. Population genetics in forensic DNA typing. *Science* 254:1745–1750.

Loerch, S. 1991. Efficacy of plastic pot scrubbers as a replacement for roughage in high-concentrate cattle diets. *Journal of Animal Science* 69:2321–2328.

Love, J. 1991. Animals in research. *Nature* 353:788.

Luzzatto, L. and, P. Goodfellow. 1989. A simple disease with no cure. *Nature* 337:17–18.

Mackenzie, D. 1990. Jumping genes confound German scientists. *New Scientist* 128:18.

Maddox, J. 1990. Understanding gel electrophoresis. *Nature* 345:381.

Mange, A.P., and E. J. Mange. 1980. *Genetics: Human aspects.* Philadelphia: Saunders College.

Marshall, E. 1995a. Gene therapy's growing pains. *Science* 269:1050–1055.

Marshall, E. 1995b. Less hype, more biology needed for gene therapy. *Science* 270:1751.

McKusick, V. A. 1986. *Mendelian inheritance in man*. Baltimore: Johns Hopkins University Press.

Mendel, G. 1866. Experiments on plant hybrids. In *The origin of genetics*, ed. Curt Stern and Eva R. Sherwood. 1966. San Francisco: W.H. Freeman.

Mendel, G. 1870. On *Hieracium*-hybrids obtained by artificial fertilization. In *Mendel's principles of heredity*, W. Bateson. 1913. Cambridge: Cambridge University Press.

Meyer, J. 1983. Die Bedeutung "hüpfender" Gene für die Ausbreitung von Antibiotika-resistenz bei Bakterien. *Schweiz. med. Wochenschrift* 113:1494–1500.

Millstone, E. et al. 1994. Plagiarism or protecting public health? *Nature* 371:647–648.

Nijhout, H. F. 1990. Metaphors and the role of genes in development. *BioEssays* 12:441–446.

Olby, R. 1994. *The path to the double helix*. New York: Dover.

Oliver, S. G. et al. 1992. The complete DNA sequence of yeast chromosome III. *Nature* 357:38–46.

O'Neill, L. et al. 1994. What are we? where did we come from? where are we going? *Science* 263:181–183.

Ow, D. et al. 1986. Transient and stable expression of the firefly luciferase gene in plant cells and transgenic plants. *Science* 234:856–859.

Portugal, F., and J. Cohen. 1978. *A century of DNA*. Cambridge: MIT Press.

Powell, B. C., and G. E. Rogers. 1990. Cyclic hair-loss and regrowth in transgenic mice overexpresssing an intermediate filament gene. *EMBO Journal* 9:1485–1493.

Pritchard, D. 1991. Modern myth. *Nature* 354:179.

Rose, S. et al. 1984. *Not in our genes*. Middlesex: Penguin.

Sarkar, S.. and A. Tauber. 1991. Fallacious claims for HGP. *Nature* 353:691.

Schroeter, C. 1926. *Das Pflanzenleben der Alpen*. Zürich: Verlag von Albert Raustein.

Schwartz, R. 1995a. Jumping genes. *The New England Journal of Medicine* 332:941–944.

Schwartz, R. 1995b. Jumping genes and the immunoglobulin V gene system. *The New England Journal of Medicine* 333:42–44.

Spitz, R. A. 1965. *The first year of life*. New York: International Universities Press.

Steiner, R. 1983. *The boundaries of natural science.* Spring Valley, N.Y.: Anthroposophic Press.

Steiner, R. 1986. *Philosophy of spiritual activity.* Hudson, N.Y.: Anthroposophic Press.

Steiner, R. 1988. *A science of knowing.* Spring Valley, N.Y.: Mercury Press.

Stone, R. 1994. Large plots are next test for transgenic crop safety. *Science* 266:1472–1473.

Straus, E. 1966. *Phenomenological psychology,* pp. 137–165. New York: Basic Books.

Stryer, L. 1988. *Biochemistry.* 3rd ed. New York: W.H. Freeman.

Sturtevant, A. H., and G.W. Beadle. 1962. An introduction to genetics. New York: Dover.

Sutton, W. S. 1903. The chromosomes in heredity. *Biological Bulletin* 4:231–251.

Suzuki, D., and P. Knudtson. 1990. *Genethics.* Cambridge: Harvard University Press.

Thompson, L. 1992. At age 2, gene therapy enters growth phase. *Science* 258:744–746.

Tonegawa, S. 1983. Somatic generation of antibody diversity. *Nature* 302:575–581.

von Frisch, K. 1974. *Animal architecture.* New York: Harcourt, Brace and Jovanovich.

Watson, J.D., and F.C. Crick. 1953. Molecular structure of nucleic acids. *Nature* 171:737–738.

Watson, J. D. et al. 1983. *Recombinant DNA.* New York: Scientific American Books, W. H. Freeman and Company.

Watson, J. D. et al. 1987. *Molecular biology of the gene.* Complete, 4th ed. Redwood City, Ca.: Benjamin-Cummings.

Weissmann, C. 1983. *Praktische Anwendungen der Gentechnik.* Umschau 1:19–22.

Wheelwright, P. 1962. *Metaphor and reality.* Bloomington: Indiana University Press.

Wheelwright, P. 1968. *The burning fountain.* Bloomington: Indiana University Press.

Whitehead, A. N. 1967. *Science and the modern world.* New York: The Free Press.

Wirz, J. 1992. Gentechnik—Gefahr oder Herausforderung? *Soziale Hygiene,* Merkblatt Nr. 144; Verein für ein erweitertes Heilwesen e.V., D-7263 Bad Liebenzell-Unterlengenhardt.

INDEX

Note: page numbers followed by "f " denote figures.

Also in This Series:

The Wholeness of Nature

*Goethe's Way toward a Science of
Conscious Participation in Nature*

by Henri Bortoft

In this major work, Henri Bortoft, a physicist and former student of David Bohm, shows how Goethe's scientific method leads to the concrete experience of wholeness in nature. In Goethe's phenomenological approach to color, for example, the generation of color is found to result from the dynamic interplay of light and darkness through which the whole circle of colors arises in meaningful order. Through active inner participation in the coming-into-being of various color phenomena, we discover their inherent interrelatedness, or wholeness.

Bortoft masterfully articulates the difference between Goethe's approach and that of mainstream science. Whereas a Goethean approach allows the phenomena themselves to speak, learning their language as it were through a direct, intuitive understanding of their interrelatedness, conventional science regards them as isolated entities to be analyzed physically and explained in terms of their material nature. Bortoft shows how Goethe's scientific method opens the way toward a dynamic, qualitative understanding of nature, thereby providing a much needed complement to the quantitative methods of modern science.

The first half of the book contains Bortoft's seminal essays *Goethe's Scientific Consciousness* and *Counterfeit and Authentic Wholes.* The second half of the work, *Understanding Goethe's Way of Science,* provides a further lively elaboration and deepening of the theme and places Goethe's scientific approach into the context of twentieth-century scientific and philosophical thought.

ISBN 0-940262-79-7 / *$24.95*

CRAIG HOLDREGE was born in Boise, Idaho, and grew up in Boulder, Colorado. He majored in philosophy at Beloit College where his interest in biology also began. He then went on to study biology and do research at the scientific research laboratory at the Goetheanum in Dornach, Switzerland. He began his career as a high school life science teacher at the Waldorf school in Wuppertal, Germany, where he taught for twelve years. For the past four years he has been teaching life sciences at the Hawthorne Valley School in Ghent, New York.

Cover art: *Die roten Rehe II*, Franz Marc, 1912.
Courtesy of Franz-Marc-Museum Kochel, Leihgabe der Bayer. Staatsgemäldesammlungen.

Cover design: Barbara Richey